Dreamweaver Advanced

Instructor's Edition

ACA Edition

MW01448338

Dreamweaver CS5: Advanced, ACA Edition

President, Axzo Press:	Jon Winder
Vice President, Product Development:	Charles G. Blum
Vice President, Operations:	Josh Pincus
Director of Publishing Systems Development:	Dan Quackenbush
Writer:	Brandon Heffernan
Copyeditor:	Catherine Oliver
Keytester:	Cliff Coryea

Trademarks

ILT Series is a trademark of Axzo Press.

Some of the product names and company names used in this book have been used for identification purposes only and may be trademarks or registered trademarks of their respective manufacturers and sellers.

Disclaimers

We reserve the right to revise this publication and make changes from time to time in its content without notice.

The Adobe Approved Certification Courseware logo is either a registered trademark or trademark of Adobe Systems Incorporated in the United States and/or other countries. The Adobe Approved Certification Courseware logo is a proprietary trademark of Adobe. All rights reserved.

The ILT Series is independent from ProCert Labs, LLC and Adobe Systems Incorporated, and are not affiliated with ProCert Labs and Adobe in any manner. This publication may assist students to prepare for an Adobe Certified Expert exam, however, neither ProCert Labs nor Adobe warrant that use of this material will ensure success in connection with any exam.

ISBN 10: 1-4260-2091-0
ISBN 13: 978-1-4260-2091-9

Printed in the United States of America

1 2 3 4 5 6 7 8 9 10 GL 13 12 11

Contents

Introduction

After reading this introduction, you'll know how to:

A Use ILT Series manuals in general.

B Use prerequisites, a target student description, course objectives, and a skills inventory to set students' expectations properly for the course.

C Set up a classroom to teach this course.

D Get support for setting up and teaching this course.

Topic A: About the manual

ILT Series philosophy

Our goal is to make you, the instructor, as successful as possible. To that end, our manuals facilitate students' learning by providing structured interaction with the software itself. While we provide text to help you explain difficult concepts, the hands-on activities are the focus of our courses. Leading the students through these activities will teach the skills and concepts effectively.

We believe strongly in the instructor-led class. For many students, having a thinking, feeling instructor in front of them is always the most comfortable way to learn. Because the students' focus should be on you, our manuals are designed and written to facilitate your interaction with the students and not to call attention to manuals themselves.

We believe in the basic approach of setting expectations, then teaching, and providing summary and review afterwards. For this reason, lessons begin with objectives and end with summaries. We also provide overall course objectives and a course summary to provide both an introduction to and closure on the entire course.

Our goal is your success. We encourage your feedback in helping us to improve our manuals continually to meet your needs.

Manual components

The manuals contain these major components:

- Table of contents
- Introduction
- Units
- Course summary
- Glossary
- Index

Each element is described below.

Table of contents

The table of contents acts as a learning roadmap for you and the students.

Introduction

The introduction contains information about our training philosophy and our manual components, features, and conventions. It contains target student, prerequisite, objective, and setup information for the specific course. Finally, the introduction contains support information.

Units

Units are the largest structural component of the actual course content. A unit begins with a title page that lists objectives for each major subdivision, or topic, within the unit. Within each topic, conceptual and explanatory information alternates with hands-on activities. Units conclude with a summary, comprising one paragraph for each topic, and an independent practice activity that gives students an opportunity to practice the skills they've learned.

The conceptual information takes the form of text paragraphs, exhibits, lists, and tables. The activities are structured in two columns, one telling students what to do, the other providing explanations, descriptions, and graphics. Throughout a unit, instructor notes are found in the left margin.

Course summary

This section provides a text summary of the entire course. It's useful for providing closure at the end of the course. The course summary also indicates the next course in this series, if there is one, and lists additional resources students might find useful as they continue to learn about the software.

Glossary

The glossary provides definitions for all of the key terms used in this course.

Index

The index at the end of this manual makes it easy for you and your students to find information about a particular software component, feature, or concept.

Manual conventions

We've tried to keep the number of elements and the types of formatting to a minimum in the manuals. We think this approach aids in clarity and makes the manuals more elegant looking. But there are some conventions and icons you should know about.

Instructor note/icon

Item	Description
Italic text	In conceptual text, indicates a new term or feature.
Bold text	In unit summaries, indicates a key term or concept. In an independent practice activity, indicates an explicit item that you select, choose, or type.
`Code font`	Indicates code or syntax.
`Longer strings of ▶ code will look ▶ like this.`	In the hands-on activities, any code that's too long to fit on a single line is divided into segments by one or more continuation characters (▶). This code should be entered as a continuous string of text.
Instructor notes.	In the left margin, provide tips, hints, and warnings for the instructor.
Select **bold item**	In the left column of hands-on activities, bold sans-serif text indicates an explicit item that you select, choose, or type.
Keycaps like ⏎ ENTER	Indicate a key on the keyboard you must press.
Warning icon.	Warnings prepare instructors for potential classroom management problems.
Tip icon.	Tips give extra information the instructor can share with students.
Setup icon.	Setup notes provide a realistic business context for instructors to share with students, or indicate additional setup steps required for the current activity.
Projector icon.	Projector notes indicate that there is a PowerPoint slide for the adjacent content.

Hands-on activities

The hands-on activities are the most important parts of our manuals. They're divided into two primary columns. The "Here's how" column gives short directions to the students. The "Here's why" column provides explanations, graphics, and clarifications. To the left, instructor notes provide tips, warnings, setups, and other information for the instructor only. Here's a sample:

Do it!

A-1:   Creating a commission formula

Take the time to make sure your students understand this worksheet. We'll be here a while.

Here's how	Here's why
1 Open Sales	This is an oversimplified sales compensation worksheet. It shows sales totals, commissions, and incentives for five sales reps.
2 Observe the contents of cell F4	F4 ▼ = =E4*C_Rate The commission rate formulas use the name "C_Rate" instead of a value for the commission rate.

For these activities, we've provided a collection of data files designed to help students learn each skill in a real-world business context. As students work through the activities, they'll modify and update these files. Of course, students might make a mistake and therefore want to re-key the activity starting from scratch. To make it easy to start over, students rename each data file at the end of the first activity in which the file is modified. Our convention for renaming files is to add the word "My" to the beginning of the file name. In the above activity, for example, students are using a file called "Sales" for the first time. At the end of this activity, they would save the file as "My sales," thus leaving the "Sales" file unchanged. If students make mistakes, they can start over using the original "Sales" file.

In some activities, however, it might not be practical to rename the data file. Such exceptions are indicated with an instructor note. If students want to retry one of these activities, you need to provide a fresh copy of the original data file.

PowerPoint presentations

Each unit in this course has an accompanying PowerPoint presentation. These slide shows are designed to support your classroom instruction while providing students with a visual focus. Each presentation begins with a list of unit objectives and ends with a unit summary slide. We strongly recommend that you run these presentations from the instructor's station as you teach this course. A copy of PowerPoint Viewer is included, so it isn't necessary to have PowerPoint installed on your computer.

The ILT Series PowerPoint add-in

The CD also contains a PowerPoint add-in that enables you to create slide notes for the class.

To load the PowerPoint add-in:

1   Copy the Course_ILT.ppa file to a convenient location on your hard drive.
2   Start PowerPoint.
3   Choose Tools, Macro, Security to open the Security dialog box. On the Security Level tab, select Medium (if necessary), and then click OK.
4   Choose Tools, Add-Ins to open the Add-Ins dialog box. Then, click Add New.
5   Browse to and double-click the Course_ILT.ppa file, and then click OK. A message box appears, warning you that macros can contain viruses.
6   Click Enable Macros. The Course_ILT add-in should now appear in the Available Add-Ins list (in the Add-Ins dialog box). The "x" in front of Course_ILT indicates that the add-in is loaded.
7   Click Close to close the Add-Ins dialog box.

After you complete this procedure, a new toolbar is available at the top of the PowerPoint window. This toolbar contains a single button labeled "Create SlideNotes." Click this button to generate slide-notes files in both text (.txt) and Excel (.xls) format. By default, these files are saved to the folder that contains the presentation. If the PowerPoint file is on a CD-ROM or in some other location to which the slide-notes files can't be saved, you'll be prompted to save the presentation to your hard drive and try again.

Topic B: Setting student expectations

Properly setting students' expectations is essential to your success. This topic will help you do that by providing:

- Prerequisites for this course
- A description of the target student
- A list of the objectives for the course
- A skills assessment for the course

Course prerequisites

Students taking this course should be familiar with personal computers and the use of a keyboard and a mouse. Furthermore, this course assumes that students have completed the following course or have equivalent experience:

- *Dreamweaver CS5: Basic, ACA Edition*

Target student

This course will benefit students who want to learn how to use Dreamweaver CS5 to create and modify Web sites. Students will learn how to design pages with CSS; work with site assets, including templates and library items; apply server-side includes; build accessible forms that validate user information; position elements and apply behaviors; add multimedia files and edit images; integrate XML-based data and transform XML with XSLT; collaborate with other developers; and verify that their sites are both usable and accessible.

Students should have basic experience with Dreamweaver CS5 and should be comfortable with defining sites, inserting elements, modifying element properties, and managing site files.

ACA certification

This course is designed to help students pass the Adobe Certified Associate (ACA) exam for Dreamweaver CS5. For complete certification training, students should complete this course and the following:

- *Dreamweaver CS5: Basic, ACA Edition*

Course objectives

You should share these overall course objectives with your students at the beginning of the day. Doing so will give the students an idea about what to expect, and it will help you identify students who might be misplaced. Students are considered misplaced when they lack the prerequisite knowledge or when they already know most of the subject matter to be covered.

Note: In addition to the general objectives listed below, specific ACA exam objectives are listed at the beginning of each topic (where applicable) and are highlighted by instructor notes throughout each unit.

After completing this course, students will know how to:

- Identify the advantages of using CSS, the difference between internal and external style sheets, and the role of inheritance and specificity in style rendering; link a page to an external style sheet; define content sections with Div tags and IDs; apply margins, padding, and border styles; arrange content sections; and use Inspect mode to explore a layout.

- Create and update library items and snippets; create and edit server-side includes; create page templates and define editable regions and attributes; create pages from templates and apply templates to pages; create and edit head elements; add keywords and descriptions; insert media files, and edit images.

- Create forms; add a variety of input fields; apply accessibility features; set the tab order of input fields; and use Spry widgets to validate form data.

- Create rollover images; apply behaviors to page elements; insert AP Divs and modify their position, size, and visibility; and dynamically control the visibility of page elements.

- Convert an HTML page to an XSLT page; bind XML data to an XSLT page; create a repeat region in an XSLT page; create dynamic links; and attach an XSLT page to an XML document.

- Use Check In and Check Out to ensure file integrity; attach design notes to files; create workflow reports; and identify and fix accessibility and usability problems.

Skills inventory

Use the following form to gauge the skill levels of the students entering the class (students have copies in the introductions of their student manuals). For each skill listed, have students rate their familiarity from 1 to 5, with five being the most familiar. Emphasize that this isn't a test. Rather, it's intended to provide students with an idea of where they're starting from at the beginning of class. If a student is wholly unfamiliar with all the skills, he or she might not be ready for the class. A student who seems to understand all of the skills, on the other hand, might need to move on to the next course in the series.

Skill	1	2	3	4	5
Linking pages to external style sheets					
Defining document sections					
Applying margins, borders, and padding					
Creating and applying ID styles					
Using Inspect mode					
Creating, inserting, and updating library items					
Creating and using snippets					
Creating, placing, and updating server-side includes					
Creating, applying, and updating page templates					
Editing head content					
Defining keywords and descriptions for a site					
Inserting multimedia content					
Editing images					
Creating forms					
Inserting form input fields					
Controlling the tab order of input fields					
Applying Spry widgets to validate user input					
Creating rollover images					
Applying the Swap Image behavior					
Inserting and manipulating AP Divs					
Controlling element visibility					
Converting an HTML page to an XSLT page					

Skill	1	2	3	4	5
Binding XML data to an XSLT page					
Creating a repeat region in an XSLT page					
Creating a dynamic link in an XSLT page					
Attaching an XSLT page to an XML page					
Checking files in and out					
Adding design notes					
Creating workflow reports					
Checking for missing Alt text					
Evaluating a site for usability and accessibility factors					

Topic C: Classroom setup

All our courses assume that each student has a personal computer to use during the class. Our hands-on approach to learning requires that they do. This topic gives information on how to set up the classroom to teach this course.

Hardware requirements

Each student's personal computer should have:

- A keyboard and a mouse
- Intel Pentium 4 or equivalent processor
- 512 MB RAM
- 1 GB of hard disk space for Dreamweaver CS5 installation; additional space needed for the operating system
- A DVD-ROM drive for installation
- A monitor set to a minimum resolution of 1280 × 960 and 24-bit color or better (Users of LCD or widescreen displays should choose the monitor's native resolution, if possible.)

Software requirements

You need the following software:

- Microsoft Windows 7, Windows Vista, or Windows XP updated with the most recent service packs
- Adobe Dreamweaver CS5
- Adobe Flash Player

Network requirements

The following network components and connectivity are also required for this course:

- Internet access, for the following purposes:
  - Updating the Windows operating system at update.microsoft.com
  - Downloading the Student Data files from www.axzopress.com (if necessary)

Classroom setup instructions

Before you teach this course, you need to perform the following steps to set up each student computer.

1 Install Windows 7 on an NTFS partition according to the software publisher's instructions. After installation is complete, if the student machines have Internet access, use Windows Update to install any critical updates and service packs.

   Note: You can also use Windows Vista or Windows XP with Service Pack 3, but the screenshots in this course were taken in Windows 7, so students' screens might look somewhat different.

2 With flat-panel displays, we recommend using the panel's native resolution for best results. Color depth/quality should be set to High (24 bit) or higher.

3   Configure Internet Explorer as follows.

   a   Click Start and choose All Programs, Internet Explorer.

   b   Configure Internet Explorer as prompted. Do not turn on Suggested Sites, and use express settings.

   c   Choose Tools, Internet Options.

   d   On the Programs tab, click Make default, and click Apply.

   e   On the Advanced tab, under Security, check "Allow active content to run in files on My Computer." Click OK.

   f   Close Internet Explorer.

4   Install Dreamweaver CS5 according to the software manufacturer's instructions.

5   Install the latest Adobe Flash Player from get.adobe.com/flashplayer. Do not install any bundled applications.

6   Display file extensions:

   a   Open Windows Explorer.

   b   (In Windows 7) Choose Organize, Folder and search options; then click the View tab.

   c   Clear the check box for "Hide extensions for known file types." Click OK.

   d   Close Windows Explorer.

7   If you have the data disc that came with this manual, locate the Student Data folder on it and copy it to the desktop of each student computer.

   If you don't have the data disc, you can download the Student Data files for the course:

   a   Connect to www.axzopress.com.

   b   Under Downloads, click Instructor-Led Training.

   c   Browse the subject categories to locate your course. Then click the course title to display a list of available downloads. (You can also access these downloads through our Catalog listings.)

   d   Click the link(s) for downloading the Student Data files. You can download the files directly to student machines or to a central location on your own network.

   e   Create a folder named Student Data on the desktop of each student computer.

   f   Double-click the downloaded zip file(s) and drag the contents into the Student Data folder.

CertBlaster exam preparation

CertBlaster pre- and post-assessment software is available for this course. To download and install this free software, students should complete the following steps:

1 Go to www.axzopress.com.

2 Under Downloads, click CertBlaster.

3 Click the link for Dreamweaver CS5.

4 Save the .EXE file to a folder on your hard drive. (**Note:** If you skip this step, the CertBlaster software will not install correctly.)

5 Click Start and choose Run.

6 Click Browse and navigate to the folder that contains the .EXE file.

7 Select the .EXE file and click Open.

8 Click OK and follow the on-screen instructions. When prompted for the password, enter **c_dwcs5**.

Topic D: Support

Your success is our primary concern. If you need help setting up this class or teaching a particular unit, topic, or activity, please don't hesitate to get in touch with us.

Contacting us

Please contact us through our Web site, www.axzopress.com. You will need to provide the name of the course, and be as specific as possible about the kind of help you need.

Instructor's tools

Our Web site provides several instructor's tools for each course, including course outlines and answers to frequently asked questions. To download these files, go to www.axzopress.com. Then, under Downloads, click Instructor-Led Training and browse our subject categories.

Unit 1

Designing with CSS

Unit time: 75 minutes

Complete this unit, and you'll know how to:

A Describe the advantages of using CSS, the difference between internal and external style sheets, and the role of inheritance and specificity in style rendering.

B Define page sections, link a page to an external style sheet, apply margins, padding, and border styles, and arrange content sections.

Topic A: Overview of style sheets

This topic covers the following Adobe ACA exam objectives for Dreamweaver CS5.

#	Objective
2.1b	Identify techniques used to maintain consistency.
2.1d	Identify benefits of using CSS styles.
2.1f	Demonstrate knowledge of fixed and flexible page sizing.
2.1h	Demonstrate knowledge of CSS best practices.
5.8c	Demonstrate knowledge of the advantages of using CSS for design.
5.8d	Demonstrate knowledge of how to use CSS starter layouts.
6.1c	Demonstrate knowledge of how to preview a Web page in a browser.

CSS

Explanation

This topic should be mostly review for students.

By itself, HTML provides limited design capability. Browsers apply default styles to many elements, such as headings, paragraphs, block quotes, and tables, but these default styles are typically not enough to achieve the design you have in mind. *Cascading Style Sheets (CSS)* is the standard style language for the Web, and you can use it to control every aspect of your Web site's appearance. CSS and HTML work together; HTML provides the basic structure, and CSS controls how the elements within that structure appear in a browser.

Style sheet types

You can apply CSS styles by using internal style sheets or external style sheets, or both. Both types of style sheet use the same syntax; the decision to use an internal or external style sheet depends on whether the styles will be applied to only a single page or to several pages.

Internal style sheets

An internal style sheet is embedded inside a page's `<head>` section, and the style rules it contains apply to only that page. Use an internal style sheet when you know that a style is needed on that one page only.

External style sheets

ACA objectives 2.1b, 2.1d, 2.1h, 5.8c

An external style sheet is a text file that contains CSS rules and is saved with a .css extension. You can link an unlimited number of pages to an external style sheet, which provides a great deal of control and efficiency. Advantages of using external style sheets include the following:

- You can create a single style rule in an external style sheet, and all pages linked to that style sheet will share the same formatting. If you need to change the formatting, you can change that style rule, rather than having to update multiple pages separately.

- You reduce the overall file size of your Web site because all of your style definitions are stored in a single location, rather than duplicated on every page. The smaller the file size of your pages, the faster those pages load in a browser, and the easier it is to perform updates.

- You can separate your style information from your content and structure. This makes your Web site more efficient, easier to maintain, and easier for search engines to index.

- The ability to control the design of multiple pages from a single style sheet saves development and maintenance time and helps prevent errors and inconsistencies.

You can use internal and external style sheets at the same time. You can place all your global styles (those that apply to multiple pages) in an external style sheet, and place your page-specific styles in internal style sheets.

Conflict resolution: The cascade

Sometimes style conflicts arise in your style sheets or across multiple style sheets. For example, if an external style sheet has a rule that makes all level-one headings blue, and one page's internal style sheet has a rule that makes all level-one headings green, the level-one headings in that page will be green, while the headings of other pages will remain blue.

The "cascading" part of Cascading Style Sheets refers to the way CSS resolves such style conflicts. The general rule is this: The closer the style rule is to the element that is being styled, the more weight the rule is given. Also, the more specific the rule, the more weight it's given.

This concept of specificity also relates to inheritance. An HTML element can inherit the CSS styles of its *parent element* (the element that contains it). For example, if you have a `<div>` tag that contains three paragraphs (`<p>` tags), and you apply font and color styles to the `<div>` tag, the three paragraphs will inherit the styles. However, if you apply a class or ID style to one of those paragraphs, and that style specifies conflicting font and color properties, they will override any inherited style values because they are more specific (more targeted) than the inherited values.

CSS starter layouts

ACA objective 5.8d

You can use CSS starter layouts to speed the development of a Web site. Dreamweaver CS5 provides several predefined style sheet layouts that you can personalize to quickly establish your site's design framework. To open a starter layout, choose File, New (or press Ctrl+N). With the Blank Page category selected, verify that HTML is selected in the Page Type list. Select the desired layout in the Layout list, and click Create. Then simply replace the default page content with your own content, and you're on your way.

Fixed and liquid layouts

ACA objective 2.1f

The Layout list in the New Document dialog box provides a variety of fixed and liquid layouts. A *fixed layout* does not change to accommodate the size of the user's browser window, while a *liquid* (or *flexible*) *layout* does. A liquid layout typically has sections with minimum widths to ensure that the intended layout is preserved in smaller browser windows. Increasing the size of the browser window stretches the layout horizontally.

Do it!

A-1: Exploring style sheets and starter layouts

Here's how	Here's why

Facilitate a brief discussion for these questions. These CSS concepts build on skills covered in the prerequisite course and should be a review for most students.

1 How do HTML and CSS work together?

HTML provides the structure of a Web page and contains all the content that appears on a page. CSS can control the way each element on a page is rendered.

2 If you wanted to apply a style to an element on one page only, should you use an internal or external style sheet? Why?

You should use an internal style sheet because the style applies to only that one page. You wouldn't want to put such a style in an external style sheet, which is meant to hold shared styles, because it would add unnecessary clutter to the style sheet.

ACA objectives 2.1d, 2.1h, 5.8c

3 What are some advantages of using an external style sheet?

Answers may vary but should include:

- *It's easier and faster to update multiple pages or individual elements in a Web site.*

- *It allows you to separate style information from content and structure, thereby making your Web site more efficient, easier to maintain, and easier for search engines to index.*

- *It reduces the overall file size of a Web site, which translates to faster download times.*

4 In your own development work, do you think you'll use more internal or external style sheets, or both? Why?

Answers may vary. For most Web sites, it makes sense to use both. You'd want to place all your global styles (styles that apply to multiple pages) in an external style sheet, and place styles that are page-specific in internal style sheets.

5 A rule in an external style sheet declares that all paragraphs should have a font size of 12 pixels. A page linked to that style sheet also contains an internal style sheet that declares that all paragraphs should be 11 pixels. On this particular page, what will the font size of paragraphs be?

Paragraphs on this page will have a font size of 11 pixels. Paragraphs on other pages linked to the external style sheet will have a font size of 12 pixels.

6 A rule for the `<body>` element in an external style sheet makes all the text on a page dark blue. Another rule in that same style sheet makes all headings dark red. But one of those headings has a class style applied to it that makes it dark gray. Describe why all of these style rules will be rendered as intended.

All elements on the page will inherit the dark blue text applied to the <body> element. However, the headings will appear dark red because the rule applied specifically to headings overrides the color inherited from the <body> element. Finally, the heading with a class applied to it is even more specific than the rule set broadly on all headings, so it takes precedence.

If the Workspace Setup dialog box appears, tell students to select Designer and click OK, and to close any other dialog boxes that appear.

7 Start Dreamweaver CS5

	8 Choose **File**, **New...**	Or press Ctrl+N.
	In the Page Type list, verify that **HTML** is selected	In the Blank Page category.
ACA objectives 2.1f, 5.8d	9 In the Layout list, select **2 column fixed**, **left sidebar**	The preview shows a gray left sidebar for navigation and a lock icon in the center of the page. This icon indicates a fixed layout—the size of the main content section will not change to accommodate the size of the user's browser window.
	Select **2 column liquid, left sidebar**	The preview shows the same left sidebar. The spring icon and percent sign indicate a liquid layout. The size of the main content section will change depending on the size of the user's browser window.
	10 Click **Create**	To open a starter page using the two-column liquid layout.
	Observe the navigation section	You can easily replace the default text with your own navigation links.
	Briefly read the default content	The content provides guidance and instructions on using the starter layout. You can replace this default content with your own content to produce a site quickly.
ACA objective 6.1c	11 Choose **File**, **Preview in Browser**, **IExplore**	To preview the page in Internet Explorer. A dialog box opens, prompting you to save the page.
	Click **Yes**	To open the Save As dialog box.
	Browse to the current topic folder	Student Data folder Unit 1\Topic A.
	In the File name box, type **My Starter Layout**	
	Click **Save**	The page opens in Internet Explorer.
	12 Point to the right edge of the browser window	The pointer changes to a two-headed arrow.
	Drag the window as far to the right as possible	Observe how the content sections stretch horizontally to accommodate the bigger window. This is an example of a liquid layout.
	13 Close the browser	
	14 In Dreamweaver, close the file	

Topic B: Page layout and global styles

This topic covers the following Adobe ACA exam objectives for Dreamweaver CS5.

#	Objective
2.1b	Identify techniques used to maintain consistency.
2.4b	Demonstrate knowledge of text formatting guidelines that improve readability.
3.1b	Demonstrate knowledge of the differences between Design view, Code view, Split view, and Live mode.
4.1b	Demonstrate knowledge of the steps for defining a new Dreamweaver site.
5.1b	Demonstrate knowledge of how to set or modify global page properties and global CSS styles, including those for text, links, and backgrounds.
5.1c	Differentiate the uses of global CSS rules and CSS rules for Div tags.
5.2a	Demonstrate knowledge of how to insert a Div tag in standard mode.
5.2b	Demonstrate knowledge of the advantages of using Div tags instead of tables for page layout.
5.2d	Demonstrate knowledge of Div tag attributes, such as height, width, margin, and padding.
5.2e	Demonstrate knowledge of how to modify Div tag attributes.
5.2g	Demonstrate knowledge of how to use external style sheets.
5.2i	Demonstrate knowledge of how to define, modify, and check CSS rules.
5.3e	Demonstrate knowledge of how to align paragraphs.
5.3j	Demonstrate knowledge of how to create a custom font stack using the Edit Font List command in the Property inspector or the font-family property in the CSS Rule Definition dialog box.
5.8c	Demonstrate knowledge of the advantages of using CSS for design.
5.8e	Demonstrate knowledge of how to use different selector types, such as descendent selectors, classes, tag selectors, pseudo class selectors, and group selectors.
5.8f	Demonstrate knowledge of how to troubleshoot CSS issues, using tools such as CSS layout backgrounds.
6.1e	Demonstrate knowledge of how to test CSS layouts across Web browsers.
6.5g	Demonstrate knowledge of using the Related Files toolbar.

Linking pages to an external style sheet

Explanation

*ACA objectives 2.1b,
5.2g, 5.8c*

To establish a consistent layout and share common styles among all your site pages, you need to create an external style sheet and link your pages to it. You can link an unlimited number of pages to an external style sheet, which provides a great deal of control and efficiency. You can update the styles and layout for multiple pages simultaneously by changing the single style sheet file.

When you're working with page sections that are used on multiple pages, such as navigation bars and copyright footers, you create your style rules in an external style sheet, rather than in internal style sheets for each applicable page. Think of an external style sheet as a repository for all of your site's global styles (styles that are shared among multiple documents, providing site-wide consistency). If multiple pages need the style, it belongs in an external style sheet. Then you link the appropriate pages to the style sheet. When you update a style in the external style sheet, it affects all pages that are linked to it.

External style sheets are text files saved with a .css extension. To link a page to an external style sheet:

1. Open the page.
2. In the CSS Styles panel, click the Attach Style Sheet button to open the Attach External Style Sheet dialog box.
3. Click Browse and navigate to the style sheet file.
4. Select the style sheet and click OK.
5. Click OK.

B-1:   Linking a page to a style sheet

The files for this activity are in Student Data folder **Unit 1\Topic B**.

Here's how	Here's why
This activity should be review for most students. 1 Choose **Site**, **New Site…**	To open the Site Setup dialog box. You'll define a site in the current topic folder.
ACA objective 4.1b 2 In the Site Name box, type **Outlander CSS**	To name the site.
Click as shown	
	To open the Choose Root Folder dialog box.
3 Click **Desktop**	On the left side of the dialog box.
Open the Student Data folder	
Open the current unit folder	
4 In the current topic folder, open the Outlander folder	
Click **Select**	To set the root folder for this site, where the files for the site will be stored.
5 Click **Save**	To define the root site folder.
6 Observe the Files panel	Outlander CSS is the site name.
In the next activity, students will wrap various sections of this page's content in <div> tags and apply ID styles to them. 7 Open index.html	(In the Files panel, double-click index.html.) This page contains content that has not yet been arranged into a layout.
ACA objective 3.1b Click ⬚ Code	(On the Document toolbar.) To switch to Code view.
Locate and observe the `<head>` section	There is no external style sheet linked to the page.
8 At the bottom of the CSS Styles panel, click 🖫	(The Attach Style Sheet button.) The Attach External Style Sheet dialog box opens.
Click **Browse**	To open the Select Style Sheet File dialog box.
ACA objective 5.2g In the styles folder, select **globalstyles**, and click **OK**	This style sheet contains some styles, but none that affect page layout.
Click **OK**	To close the Attach External Style Sheet dialog box and link the page to globalstyles.css.

Point out the line number where the link tag appears.

9	Observe the `<head>` section	The `<link>` tag is added to the `<head>` section, linking the document to the style sheet.
10	Click [Design]	To switch to Design view. Some of the text is formatted, but the overall layout of the page is disorganized. You'll continue to work on this page in the next activity.
11	Press [CTRL] + [S]	To save your changes.

Defining page sections

Explanation

Page layouts are typically divided into distinct sections. For example, many Web pages have a banner or a navigation bar at the top of the page and have sections or columns of information below, as illustrated in Exhibit 1-1.

ACA objectives 2.1b, 5.1c, 5.2b, 5.8c

Dividing a layout into distinct sections makes it easier to arrange each section on the page and to control styles within each section. If you use the same basic page layout for multiple pages, as most Web sites do, defining separate content sections is vital to producing a consistent and efficient layout. Controlling a layout with CSS is efficient because the style and positioning rules are stored in an external style sheet that's shared by multiple pages. Therefore, less code is required to achieve a particular layout, and there's no need to duplicate styles in each page. You can use Div tags to define document sections.

Exhibit 1-1: A page divided into distinct sections

Divs and IDs

ACA objectives 5.1c, 5.2b, 5.8c

The best way to define page sections is to use Div tags and IDs. The `<div>` (division) tag acts as a generic container for page elements. You can use it to define various page sections, such as navigation bars, content areas, and footers, and then give each section a logically named ID to augment your document structure. You can then apply styles to each ID to control the page layout. This method of page layout is superior to using tables because it involves less page code and is therefore more efficient. It also provides more precise control over layouts than tables can provide, and the layouts are typically easier to update.

For example, Exhibit 1-2 shows the code used to define a section of content in a layout. All elements in the section are wrapped in a Div tag with the ID `columnLeft`. You can create a CSS rule that selects `#columnLeft` (in other words, a rule that uses the ID name as a selector). You can then arrange and format all of the contained elements as a single object.

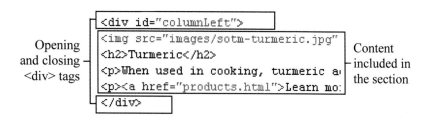

Opening and closing <div> tags

Content included in the section

Exhibit 1-2: Content wrapped in a Div tag

Do it!

B-2: Discussing page sections and global styles

Questions and answers

ACA objective 5.1c

1 What's the role of a Div tag?

The <div> (division) tag acts as a generic container for page elements. If you apply certain styles to a Div tag, any content in the Div will share those styles.

ACA objectives 2.1b, 5.2b, 5.8c

2 What are some advantages of using Div tags and IDs to create a page layout?

Answers may vary. Wrapping content in Div tags enables you to name each section with an ID, and this practice can help make your document structure meaningful and easier to update. It also enables you to apply different CSS styles to each section.

3 How do IDs help make your document structure more meaningful?

Dividing a page into different sections with unique IDs allows you to give meaningful names to each section, such as "Header," "Navigation," "MainContent," "footer," and so forth. These names can make your pages easier to read and update for other developers.

ACA objective 2.1b

4 How can using Div tags and IDs to define page sections help you to maintain consistency across the pages in your site?

You can use Div tags and IDs to define major content sections on every page so that each page shares the same design framework. When you change ID styles, all pages linked to the style sheet are updated simultaneously.

Applying Div tags

Explanation

You can create an empty Div tag and then add content to it, or you can wrap a Div tag around existing content. When inserting a Div tag, you might find it easier to work in Code view for precise placement of the insertion point. You can also enter the HTML code manually, if you prefer.

ACA objective 5.2a

To insert a new Div tag:

1   (Optional) Switch to Code view.
2   Click to place the insertion point where you want the Div tag to begin.
3   In the Insert panel, click the Insert Div Tag button to open the Insert Div Tag dialog box.
4   In the Insert list, verify that "At insertion point" is selected.
5   (Optional) Select a Class or ID to apply to the tag. (If no class or ID styles exist, these drop-down lists are empty.)
6   Click OK.
7   Delete the sample text that Dreamweaver inserts in the Div tag.

If you're working with a page that already has content, you can wrap a Div tag around various sections as needed. To wrap a Div tag around a section of content:

1   Select the content in Code view or Design view.
2   In the Insert panel, click Insert Div Tag to open the Insert Div Tag dialog box.
3   In the Insert list, verify that "Wrap around selection" is selected.
4   (Optional) Select a Class or ID.
5   Click OK.

Applying a class or ID to a Div tag

ACA objective 5.2e

If you like to work in Design view and you want to apply a class style or ID style to a Div tag, first create the style so that you can select it from the Class or ID list in the Property inspector or the Insert Div Tag dialog box. If you haven't yet created the style you want to use, you can open the Insert Div Tag dialog box and click New CSS Style to define a new class or ID style.

Switching between page code and a style sheet

ACA objective 6.5g

You can use the Related Files toolbar to quickly switch between your page code and your style sheet. The Related Files toolbar lists all of the files to which the current page is linked. The example in Exhibit 1-3 shows one related file, the external style sheet globalstyles.css. (The Source Code button refers to the code of the current document.) You can click any file name on the Related Files toolbar to open that file for editing.

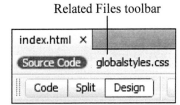

Exhibit 1-3: The Related Files toolbar

HTML comments

When you need to work in Code view, use HTML comments to organize and label your document structure. HTML comments are like notes to yourself and other developers, indicating such things as where a section begins or ends, what a specific section of code is meant for, who was the last person to edit the code, and so forth. Comments can help you visually scan the code to find an area that you're looking for.

The syntax for an HTML comment is as follows:

```
<!-- Your comment text -->
```

HTML comments do not appear as text on the Web page.

To insert a comment, you can type the comment code and text, or you can click the Apply Comment button on the Coding toolbar and choose Apply HTML Comment. The insertion point is then placed inside the comment tags so you can begin typing your text.

Do it!

B-3: Defining document sections

Here's how	Here's why

ACA objective 6.5g

1 Click **globalstyles.css**

(On the Related Files toolbar.) To open the style sheet in Split view.

Present this activity as if students had already created the ID styles and will now apply them to various document sections.

Scroll to the bottom of the code

Observe the existing ID styles — This style sheet contains some styles that use ID selectors. You will apply each of these styles to a `<div>` tag.

2 Click **Source Code** — (On the Related Files toolbar.) To switch to index.html in Split view.

Switch to Code view

3 Locate the HTML comments — (Comments appear as gray text in Code view.) Comments are notes that you can insert into your code to make it easier to find and understand particular code blocks.

4 Click to place the insertion point before the first link tag, as shown

You'll insert a `<div>` tag that will hold the Outlander logo.

5 Click where shown

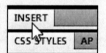

To expand the Insert panel.

ACA objective 5.2a

6 In the Insert panel, click ▦ — (The Insert Div Tag button.) To open the Insert Div Tag dialog box.

In the Insert list, verify that **At insertion point** is selected

ACA objective 5.2e

Tell students that any Class or ID style they create will appear in these lists.

From the ID list, select **logo** — This style sets the Outlander logo as a background image. Later, you'll examine the style more closely.

Click **OK** — Dreamweaver automatically inserts placeholder text inside the Div.

⚠ *Be sure that students don't delete the closing tag.*

7 Press ⬚DELETE⬚ — To delete the placeholder text.

| | 8 | Switch to Design view | The logo appears at the top of the page. The `<div>` tag you inserted has an ID named "logo." This style makes the image logo.gif a background for the `<div>` tag. |

Facilitate a brief discussion.

ACA objectives 5.1b, 2.1b, 5.2b, 5.8c

9 Why might you want to insert an image by using a style sheet?

If you insert an image as a background of an element via a style sheet, rather than using the `<img>` tag to embed an image in the code, you can set which image is used from the style sheet. This approach is useful for images that appear on multiple pages; you can update the image used in these pages by simply changing the style sheet rather than changing each document.

10 Switch to Code view

If students have changed the code in other ways, line 14 might not be accurate. Tell them to select the code between the div and the "End masthead section" comment.

In the column of line numbers, click **14**, and observe the selection

```
12          <!-- Begin masthead section:
13          <div id="logo"></div>
14 ☐  <a href="index.html">home</a> |
          locations</a> | <a href="product
     ☐  href="mailto:info@outlanderspice
15          <!-- End masthead section-->
```

All the code on line 14 is selected. You'll enclose these links in a new Div section and then apply an ID style to it.

11 In the Insert panel, click ▦   To insert a new Div.

Observe the Insert list

Because you selected a block of code, "Wrap around selection" is automatically selected.

Point out that the ID "logo" isn't available anymore because ID styles can be used only once per page.

From the ID list, select **globalNav**

Click **OK**   Dreamweaver wraps a Div with the id "globalNav" around the selection.

Mention that the dotted lines are a default visual aid to help distinguish layout sections.

12 Switch to Design view   To view the changes. Wrapping the navigation links in a Div with the "globalNav" style applies a green background color, plus text and spacing properties. The dotted lines are a visual aid.

Switch to Code view

Tell students that their line numbers might be slightly different.

13 Drag over the line numbers needed to select all of the code between the "left column" comments

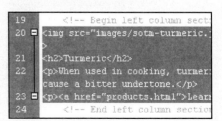

```
19          <!-- Begin left column sect:
20 ☐ <img src="images/sotm-turmeric.:
     >
21  <h2>Turmeric</h2>
22  <p>When used in cooking, turmer:
    cause a bitter undertone.</p>
23 ☐ <p><a href="products.html">Learı
24          <!-- End left column sectio:
```

Your line numbers might be slightly different from those shown here.

ACA objective 5.2a

14 Wrap the selection in a Div and apply the ID **columnLeft**

Switch to Design view

This ID style places the Div and its contents on the left side of the page.

Some of the content overlaps. You'll fix this by applying a Div tag and an ID style that formats the remaining content into separate columns.

Help students with this selection, if necessary.

15 Select all of the code between the "center column" comments

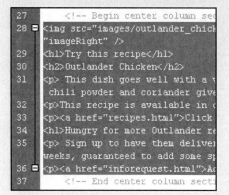

Switch to Code view and scroll down to access the code.

Remind students that after they apply an ID style, it no longer appears in the list.

Wrap the selection in a Div and apply the ID **columnCenter**

16 Select all of the code between the "right column" comments

Scroll down to access the code.

Wrap the selection in a Div and apply the ID **columnRight**

Help students locate the comments.

17 Select everything between "content section" comments

(From about line 18 to line 48.) The content section contains all of the code for the right, center, and left column <div> tags.

Wrap the selection in a Div and apply the ID **content**

18 Switch to Design view

Point out that the layout still has a few problems that students will solve in the next activity.

Click the page

To deselect the content. The content sections are arranged into separate columns according to the ID styles you applied. However, the page still has a few design issues that you'll continue to work on in the next activity.

19 Save your changes

Press Ctrl+S.

Modifying CSS rules

Explanation

You can modify your CSS rules by using the CSS Rule Definition dialog box, which organizes CSS styles into several categories, as shown in Exhibit 1-4. Each category contains a set of related style definitions.

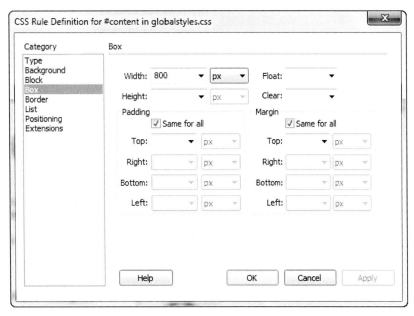

Exhibit 1-4: The CSS Rule Definition dialog box with the Box category selected

ACA objective 5.2i

To edit a CSS rule, double-click it in the CSS Styles panel; then edit the definitions in the CSS Rule Definition dialog box. You can also edit styles manually in Code view or Split view.

The Box model

ACA objectives 5.2d, 5.2e

The *Box model* is the layout model of CSS. Every rendered HTML element creates a box. The styles of the Box model are those that directly influence the appearance of an element's box: its height, width, borders, padding, and margins.

For example, assume that the text "Element content" in Exhibit 1-5 is defined by a level-one heading (an `<h1>` tag). The solid line around the text represents its border, and the space between the content and the border is the element's *padding*. An element's *margin* is the space between its border and adjacent elements. You can control these and other styles by setting values in the Box category of the CSS Rule Definition dialog box.

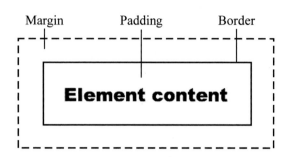

Exhibit 1-5: The Box model

Viewing margins and padding in Design view

Dreamweaver provides a visual aid to help you distinguish between margins and padding while you work on a page layout. Margins are indicated with thick crosshatched lines, and padding is indicated with thin crosshatched lines. To enable or disable this visual aid, click the Visual Aids button and choose CSS Layout Box Model.

Do it!

B-4: Controlling margins, padding, and borders

Here's how	Here's why
1 Observe the "Did you know?" column	(The section with the green background color.) The top of this Div section is flush with the bottom of the navigation bar. However, the other two columns have space between them and the navigation bar.
2 In the CSS Styles panel, click **All**	(If necessary.) To display all CSS rules associated with the current document.
3 Scroll down and double-click **#columnRight**	(In the CSS Styles panel.) You'll apply a top margin to this column to align it with the other two columns.
4 In the Category list, select **Box**	To display the Box-model styles, which include an element's height, width, padding, and margins.
5 Observe the Padding values	The "Same for all" check box indicates that the selected element has the same padding values on all four sides.

Tell students they can use the dotted lines to determine how each Div section is arranged.

ACA objectives 5.2d, 5.2e, 5.2i

Point out that this element already has 10 pixels of padding on all four sides.

6	Under Margin, clear **Same for all**	You'll apply a margin value to only one side of this Div.
	In the Top box, enter **10**	
	Verify that **pixels (px)** is selected	This is the default unit of measurement.
	Click **OK**	The right column now aligns with the other two columns. (The other columns already have a 10-pixel top margin applied.)
7	Click the text **Did you know?**	To place the insertion point.
	In the Tag selector, click **<div#columnRight>**	To select the Div section for observation. Notice that the top margin is indicated by the thick crosshatched lines. The padding (on all four sides of the box) is indicated by the thin crosshatched lines.
8	Click in the navigation bar	
	In the Tag selector, click **<div#globalNav>**	The navigation bar has a small amount of padding applied to it already. You'll increase the padding values on all four sides.
9	In the CSS Styles panel, double-click **#globalNav**	To open the CSS Rule Definition dialog box.
	Select the **Box** category	
	Move the dialog box so that you can see the navigation bar	(If necessary.) You'll observe the changes you make without closing the dialog box.
10	Under Padding, edit the Top box to read **8**	To increase the padding on all four sides of the globalNav element.
	Click **Apply**	To apply the style changes without closing the dialog box.
11	Select the **Border** category	
	Under Style, clear **Same for all**	
	From the Top list, select **solid**	You'll apply a solid border to the top of the navigation bar.
12	For the Width property, clear **Same for all**	
	In the Top box, type **6**	To set the border width to 6 pixels.

Tell students to apply a dark green color such as #060.

13	For the Color property, clear **Same for all**	
	Click the **Top** box and select a dark green color	
	Click **Apply**	To apply the border to the top of the navigation bar.
	Click **OK**	To close the dialog box.
14	Observe the space between the left and center columns	There's no space between these adjacent Div sections.
	In the CSS Styles panel, double-click **#columnCenter**	You'll edit the #columnCenter style.
	In the Box category, apply a left margin of **20** pixels	Select the Box category and then type 20 in the Left box, under Margin.
	Click **OK**	
15	Double-click **#columnLeft**	(In the CSS Styles panel.) You'll apply padding and a border to one side of this element.
	In the Box category, apply **14** pixels of padding to the right side	Clear "Same for all" and type 14 in the Right box.
	Apply **6** pixels of padding to the left side	In the Left box, type 6.
16	In the Border category, under Style, clear **Same for all**	
	From the Right list, select **double**	To apply a double border to the right side of this Div section.
	For the Width property, clear **Same for all**	
	Under Width, in the Right box, type **3**	To set the border width to 3 pixels.
17	For the Color property, clear **Same for all**	
	Under Color, in the Right box, select a dark gray color	
	Click **OK**	To apply the styles and close the dialog box.

Or press F12.

18	Choose **File**, **Preview in Browser**, **IExplore**	Or press F12.
	Click **Yes**	To save your changes.
	Verify the results and make changes if necessary	In the next activity, you'll create a CSS rule to format the copyright text.
	Close the browser	

Creating ID styles

Explanation

When you create a CSS rule in Dreamweaver, you can select one of four selector types in the New CSS Rule dialog box. The four types are Class, ID, Tag, and Compound. *Selectors* identify the element(s) to which the style properties will be applied.

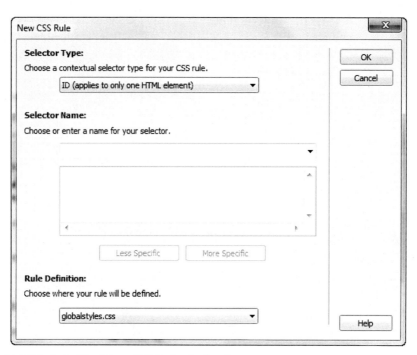

Exhibit 1-6: The New CSS Rule dialog box

ACA objectives 5.2i, 5.8e

ID styles must be unique; they can be applied only once per page. If the pages in your site have a consistent navigation bar, you can define that section with a Div tag with an ID that logically names or describes the section, such as "navbar." Then you apply a CSS rule to it by using an ID selector.

To create an ID style:

1 Open a style sheet or a Web page that's linked to a style sheet.
2 In the CSS Styles panel, click the New CSS Rule button.
3 In the New CSS Rule dialog box, under Selector type, select Advanced.
4 In the Selector box, enter an ID name for the rule. An ID must begin with the # sign.
5 Under Define in, do one of the following:
   • From the list, select a style sheet or select New Style Sheet File.
   • Select "This document only" (to insert the rule in the current document).
6 Click OK.
7 In the CSS Rule Definition dialog box, specify the properties for the style.
8 Click OK.

Floating and clearing elements

Floating is a CSS layout method that allows you to arrange content into columns. When you float an element, the element becomes a box and you must specify a width value. For example, say you have an element with a width of 400 pixels, and a paragraph of text follows it. If you float this element to the left, the text that follows it will wrap to its opposite side, as shown in Exhibit 1-7. If you float element A to the right, the text beneath it will wrap around the other side.

```
ELEMENT A (float:left)          "Lorem ipsum dolor sit amet, consectetur
                                 adipisicing elit, sed do eiusmod tempor
incididunt ut labore et dolore magna aliqua. Ut enim ad minim veniam, quis nostrud
exercitation ullamco laboris nisi ut aliquip ex ea commodo consequat. Duis aute irure
dolor in reprehenderit in voluptate velit esse cillum dolore eu fugiat nulla pariatur.
Excepteur sint occaecat cupidatat non proident, sunt in culpa qui officia deserunt
mollit anim id est laborum."
```

Exhibit 1-7: An element (A) floated to the left

For another example, if you have two elements that are floated to the left, you can create a two-column effect, as shown in Exhibit 1-8.

```
ELEMENT A (float:left)          ELEMENT B (float:left)             "Lorem
                                                                    ipsum
dolor sit amet, consectetur adipisicing elit, sed do eiusmod tempor incididunt ut
labore et dolore magna aliqua. Ut enim ad minim veniam, quis nostrud exercitation
ullamco laboris nisi ut aliquip ex ea commodo consequat. Duis aute irure dolor in
reprehenderit in voluptate velit esse cillum dolore eu fugiat nulla pariatur. Excepteur
sint occaecat cupidatat non proident, sunt in culpa qui officia deserunt mollit anim id
est laborum."
```

Exhibit 1-8: Two elements floated to the left

Notice that the float also affects the text that follows element B. The text still wraps around the floated element in as much space is available. If this is not the desired effect, and you don't want an element to be affected by a floated element, you can use the `clear` property. In this same example, if you apply the `clear` property to the left side of the paragraph, it prevents any floated element from appearing on its left side, as shown in Exhibit 1-9. You can also clear an element to the right side or both sides.

```
ELEMENT A (float:left)          ELEMENT B (float:left)
"Lorem ipsum dolor sit amet, consectetur adipisicing elit, sed do eiusmod tempor
incididunt ut labore et dolore magna aliqua. Ut enim ad minim veniam, quis nostrud
exercitation ullamco laboris nisi ut aliquip ex ea commodo consequat. Duis aute irure
dolor in reprehenderit in voluptate velit esse cillum dolore eu fugiat nulla pariatur.
Excepteur sint occaecat cupidatat non proident, sunt in culpa qui officia deserunt
mollit anim id est laborum."
```

Exhibit 1-9: Two left-floated elements and a cleared paragraph

Visual aids for Div-based layouts

ACA objective 5.8f

When you're working in a Div-based layout, you might find it helpful to use visual aids. For example, you can use the CSS Layout Backgrounds visual aid to color-code your Div tag sections, making it easier to identify each section in a box layout. These colors appear only in Dreamweaver as a development aid and are not actually applied to the content or style sheet. This and other visual aids can help you troubleshoot a layout and arrange elements precisely.

Text styles and page layout

ACA objective 2.4b

Sometimes the text styles you choose—font sizes in particular—can affect your page layout. For example, if you create a layout that consists of several narrow columns and you then apply a large font size, you can end up with content sections that have too few words on each line of text, which can make the content difficult to read. For this reason, it can be helpful to set your preferred fonts and font sizes before you establish the widths of your content sections. The readability of your content is critical, so be sure to consider your fonts, font sizes, alignments, and indents before you finalize the dimensions of your content regions.

Custom font combinations

ACA objectives 2.1b, 5.3j

You can use the Edit Font List command to customize the font combinations that are displayed in the Font list in the Property inspector. The Font list contains several predefined font combinations based on some of the most commonly available fonts.

These font combinations help to ensure that your text is displayed consistently in a variety of browsers and operating systems. Some users might not have certain fonts that you declare, so it's important to specify several similar fonts that are common to various operating systems. Browsers will attempt to display the first font in a list. If the user's computer does not have that font installed, the browser attempts to apply the next font in the list, and so on.

To create a custom font combination that will appear in the Font list in the Property inspector:

1 Select the CSS category in the Property inspector.
2 Open the Font list and select Edit Font List.
3 In the Edit Font List dialog box, select a font in the Available fonts list and click the left-pointing arrow button to add the font to the Chosen fonts list.
4 Repeat step 3 to add as many fonts as needed, and then click OK.

If you want to add a font that does not appear in your Available fonts list, type the font's name in the box below the Available fonts list and then click the left-pointing arrow button to add it to the Chosen fonts list.

Do it!

B-5:   Creating and applying an ID style

Here's how	Here's why

In the previous activity, students applied ID styles to document sections. Now students will create an ID style to format the copyright text at the bottom of the page.

ACA objective 5.2i

1 In the CSS Styles panel, click 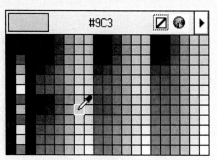   (The New CSS Rule button.) To open the New CSS Rule dialog box.

From the Selector Type list, select **ID**

In the Selector name box, type **copyright**   To create an ID rule named "copyright." (If you leave out the # at the beginning of the selector name, Dreamweaver adds it automatically.)

ACA objective 5.2g

Under Rule Definition, verify that **globalstyles.css** is selected   You'll save this rule in the external style sheet.

Point out that the selector appears in the CSS Styles panel.

Click **OK**   To open the CSS Rule Definition dialog box. Notice that the style name appears in the CSS Styles panel and the dialog box.

ACA objective 5.1b

2 In the Type category, in the Font-size box, type **10**   To make the font size 10 pixels. (Pixels are the default unit of measurement.)

From the Font-style list, select **italic**

From the Font-weight list, select **bold**

3 In the Background category, click the Background color box   A color palette appears, and the pointer changes to an eyedropper.

Tell students that the number sign associated with colors has nothing to do with the number sign associated with ID selectors.

Select the green color **#9C3**, as shown

To apply a green background color to the copyright section.

ACA objectives 2.4b, 5.3e

4 In the Block category, from the Text-align list, select **center**   To center the copyright text.

5 In the Box category, from the Clear list, select **both**

Applying the `clear` property to an element prevents another element from floating to one or both sides. In this case, selecting "both" causes the element to appear below the three columns because they all have a `float` property applied to them.

6 Apply 6 pixels of padding on all four sides

In the Box category, under Padding, verify that "Same for all" is selected, and type 6 in the Top box.

Click **OK**

7 Switch to Code view

Next, you need to apply the ID style to the copyright text for it to take effect.

8 In the copyright section, select the copyright text

```
51          <!-- Begin copyright sectio
52 ⊟ Copyright Outlander Spices 2008
53          <!-- End copyright section
```

At the bottom of the page.

Wrap it in a Div and apply the **copyright** ID to it

Click the Insert Div Tag button, select copyright from the ID list, and click OK.

9 Switch to Design view

Deselect and observe the copyright text

(Scroll down.) The copyright section is formatted with the styles you set for the copyright ID.

10 On the Document toolbar, click

To display the Visual Aids list.

From the list, select **CSS Layout Backgrounds**

To color-code the Div sections. The colors make it easier to identify sections in box layouts. These colors appear only in Dreamweaver as a development aid and are not actually applied to the content or style sheet.

Disable the visual aid

From the Visual Aids list, select CSS Layout Backgrounds again.

11 Disable the CSS Layout Outlines visual aid

To turn off the default dashed lines around each Div section.

12 Save the page and preview it in Internet Explorer

Click Yes if prompted to save changes in the style sheet.

Close the browser

Inspect mode

Explanation

In a layout with various elements and content regions that all have their own box properties, such as margins and padding, it can be difficult to determine which element you need to change to achieve a particular layout adjustment. By using Inspect mode, you can quickly determine which element you need to modify to achieve a desired outcome.

Live View and Live Code view

ACA objectives 5.2i, 6.1e

When you switch to Inspect mode, Live View is activated automatically, and Dreamweaver displays a message stating that Inspect mode works best with specific interface settings. Click "Switch now" to activate those settings. This action also enables Live Code view and opens the CSS Styles panel in Current mode.

When Inspect mode is enabled, you can quickly view an element's CSS Box model properties simply by pointing to the element. Different highlight colors are displayed for an element's margins, padding, borders, and content area. The CSS Styles panel changes to show the properties for the element you're pointing to, and the code for the selected element is highlighted in the split Live Code view pane. If you click a page element, you lock in the selection. Click the Inspect button again to re-activate the live selection feature.

Together, these interface features enable you to quickly view an element's CSS properties while simultaneously locating the relevant code. This can save you a lot of time because you won't need to scroll around looking for individual elements or properties that you need to verify or modify.

Do it!

B-6: Using Inspect mode to explore a layout

The files for this activity are in Student Data folder **Unit 1\Topic B**.

Here's how	Here's why
Index.html is open in Design view.	
1 On the Document toolbar, click [Inspect]	To switch to Inspect mode.
2 Point to different page elements	When you point to a page element in Inspect mode, the element's height and width are indicated by a teal color, the padding is shown as teal, and element margins are yellow. This color coding can help you to quickly determine which element you need to modify to achieve a particular layout adjustment.
3 Read the message under the Document toolbar	
4 Click **Switch now**	To optimize the interface for Inspect mode. Live Code is activated in Split view, and the CSS Styles panel opens in Current mode.
5 In the Design view pane, scroll to the right	
6 Point to **Did you know?**	The HTML for the heading is displayed in Live Code view, and the CSS Styles panel shows the style properties affecting only that element.
7 Point above the heading, as shown	

ACA objectives 5.2i, 6.1e

If a message bar appears about a Netscape/Firefox plug-in, tell students to ignore it.

To select the Div that defines this column of content.

In the HTML, verify that the **columnRight** Div is selected	
Click to lock in the selection	Observe how the information changes in the CSS Styles panel. The Div's margin is indicated by a pale yellow, and the padding is shown as lavender. You added the top margin earlier.
8 In the CSS Styles panel, scroll down to view the padding property	If necessary.
9 Click **10px**	To select it for editing.
Type **14** and press (↵ ENTER)	To increase the padding for this element. You can see the change indicated by the increased area of the padding color.

Help students with this step, if necessary. If they select the wrong thing, tell them to re-activate Inspect mode.

10	Click anywhere on the page	To turn off Inspect mode.
11	Switch to Design view	
	Turn off Live View	Click the Live View button.
12	Save and close all open files	

Unit summary: Designing with CSS

Topic A   In this topic, you learned about some of the advantages of using CSS. You learned how HTML and CSS work together to establish a page's design, and you identified the difference between **internal** and **external style sheets** and when you would use each kind.

Topic B   In this topic, you learned how to define page sections by using **Div tags** and **IDs**, and how to attach an external style sheet to a page. You also learned about the **Box model**, and you learned how to apply **borders**, **margins**, and **padding**. Finally, you learned how to arrange content sections by applying the **float** and **clear** properties, and you learned how to quickly view and modify CSS styles by using **Inspect mode**.

Independent practice activity

In this activity, you'll attach an external style sheet to a page. Then you'll define content sections with `<div>` tags and IDs. Finally, you'll modify a CSS rule and view the results.

The files for this activity are in Student Data folder **Unit 1\Unit summary**.

1   Define a new site named **CSS practice**, using the Outlander folder as your local root folder (within the Unit summary folder).

2   From the Files panel, open index.html.

3   Attach the globalstyles.css style sheet to the page. (*Hint:* The style sheet is in the styles folder.)

4   Select the chilies image and wrap it in a Div tag. Give the Div the ID **chilis**. Then create a CSS rule. From the Selector Type list, select **ID**. In the Selector Name box, type **#chilis**, and then click OK. Float the image to the left.

5   Switch to Code view, and select the first two paragraphs (between the chilis image and the NEWS SECTION comment). Wrap the selection in a Div tag and give it the ID **intro**.

6   Create a CSS rule using **#intro** as the selector. (Dreamweaver automatically makes #intro the default selector in the New CSS Rule dialog box.) Then, give the Div a width of 350 pixels, float it to the left, and give it a left margin of 20 pixels and a top margin of 10 pixels.

7   Switch to Design view to verify the results.

8   Switch to Code view and select all content between the NEWS SECTION comment and the COPYRIGHT comment. Wrap the content in a Div tag and give it the ID **news**.

9   Create a CSS rule for #news that clears all content from its left side. Also, float the Div to the left, and give it a width of 565 pixels, a left margin of 50 pixels, a bottom margin of 30 pixels, and 10 pixels of top padding.

10   Preview the page in your browser. The finished results should look similar to the example in Exhibit 1-10.

11   Close the browser, and close all open files.

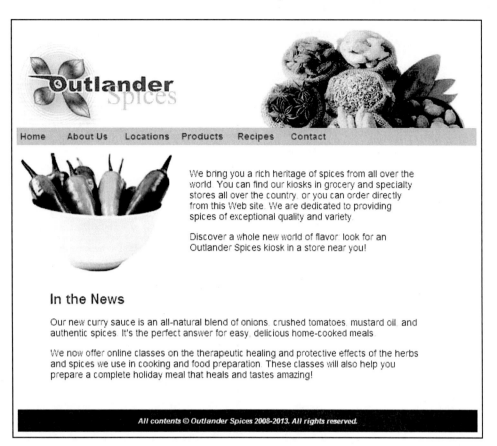

Exhibit 1-10: The completed page

Review questions

1 Structuring your documents in a meaningful, logical hierarchy of elements provides which of the following benefits? [Choose all that apply.]

   A It helps to establish consistency throughout a page or a site.

   B It saves you time and effort when you later update a site.

   C It allows your pages to be indexed by search engines more efficiently.

   D It increases your site traffic.

   E It allows Dreamweaver to function optimally.

2 You should place a CSS style rule in an internal style sheet if:

   A You want the rule to help establish consistency across multiple pages.

   B You need the rule to apply to an element on that page only.

   C You need the rule to apply to several individual pages, but not to all of the pages in the site.

   D You want the rule to be ignored in Dreamweaver but applied in a browser.

3 If you want to apply a CSS rule to all instances of a particular HTML element, what selector type should you specify in the New CSS Rule dialog box?

   A Class

   B Tag

   C Advanced

   D ID

4 Which style properties are part of the Box model of CSS? [Choose all that apply.]

   A Borders

   B Padding

   C Font size

   D Background color

   E Margins

5 True or false? If you want to arrange page elements by using the `float` property, you must give those page elements explicit width values.

   True

6 You use an ID selector if:

   A You want to define the styles for a content section that appears only once on a page.

   B You want to define the styles for a content section that appears more than once on a page.

   C The element you're applying it to is a `<div>`.

   D The element you're applying it to is *not* a `<div>`.

Unit 2

Site assets

Unit time: 90 minutes

Complete this unit, and you'll know how to:

A Work with library items, and create and apply snippets and server-side includes.

B Create templates, editable regions, and editable attributes; create a page from a template; and apply a template to an existing page.

C Create and edit `<head>` elements, and add keywords and a description to a page.

D Work with Flash files and edit images.

Topic A: Library assets, snippets, and includes

This topic covers the following Adobe ACA exam objectives for Dreamweaver CS5.

#	Objective
2.1b	Identify techniques used to maintain consistency.
3.4b	Identify types of content that can be accessed by using the Assets panel.
3.4c	Demonstrate knowledge of how to apply assets from the Assets panel to a Web page.

Working with library assets

Explanation

A *library* is a special Dreamweaver file in which you can store assets for your Web pages, such as text, images, or Flash files. When you place an asset in a library, it's easy to reuse it multiple times in your site. If you change a library item, all instances of that item are updated automatically. This feature can save you a lot of time and effort in the development process, especially if you're working with files that are not finalized.

ACA objectives 2.1b, 3.4b

For example, if you want a special message to appear on multiple pages, you can type the text, select it, and add it to the library. Then you can drag that item from the library onto the desired pages, and the same text will appear. If you update the text in the library, all instances of the text are updated automatically; you don't have to modify any individual pages. This is similar to the way a style sheet allows you to update multiple pages from a single source.

For page elements that are linked, such as images or any other external resource pulled into the document, the library item only stores the path to that element. Therefore, the file must remain in its original location.

Library items are displayed in the Assets panel, as shown in Exhibit 2-1. To work with library items, activate the Assets panel and click the Library button (the book icon) on the left side of the panel.

Exhibit 2-1: A library item in the Assets panel

Library items are stored in a folder named Library, in your site's root folder. This folder is created automatically when you first add a library item. Each site you create has its own unique library.

A-1:   Creating and inserting a library item

Here's how	Here's why
1 Choose **Site, New Site...**	To open the Site Setup dialog box. You must define a site before you can use the Assets panel.
2 In the Site Name box, type **Outlander assets**	To name the site.
3 Browse to the current topic folder	Student Data folder Unit 2\Topic A.
Open the Outlander folder, click **Select**, and then click **Save**	To set the root folder for this site and create the site.
4 Open index.html	(Double-click it in the Files panel.) You'll create a library item that you can reuse.
5 Next to the Files panel tab, click **Assets**	To open the Assets panel. (You can also choose Window, Assets.)
Click 📖	(The Library button.) To activate the library section of the Assets panel. The library is empty.
6 On the page, click the green spice shaker image, as shown	 To select it.
7 At the bottom of the Assets panel, click 🔁	(The New Library Item button.) The graphic appears in the preview pane, and an untitled library item appears in the list.
8 Type **Spice shaker graphic** and press (← ENTER)	To name the library item.
9 Activate the Files panel	A folder named Library has been added to the site folder. The Library folder contains the Spice shaker graphic.lbi file you created. You'll add the library item to another page.
10 Open recipes.html	From the Files panel.
11 Click below the first recipe, as shown	 To place the insertion point. You'll insert the library item here.

12 Activate the Assets panel	
Select the Spice shaker graphic library item	
Click [Insert]	(At the bottom of the Assets panel.) To add the library item. You can also drag a library item onto the page.
13 Deselect the image	(Click anywhere on the page.) The image is highlighted to indicate that it's a library item.
14 Save the page and preview it in Internet Explorer	The highlighting appears only in Dreamweaver.
Close the browser	
15 Describe a benefit of using library items	*Updating is streamlined. If you update an item in the library, all instances of that item are updated automatically; you don't have to modify any individual pages.*

ACA objective 3.4c

Tell students they can also drag an item onto the page.

Tell students that they can use the Preferences dialog box to change the highlighting color for library items.

Updating library items

Explanation

When you insert a library item, the item itself isn't inserted on the page. Instead, Dreamweaver inserts a copy of the HTML code for that item on the page. The code also includes an HTML comment that refers to the library item. Remember, each instance of a library item is a reference to the original library item, so you can update all instances used throughout the site simply by updating the original library item. This feature can be useful if you have resources that change often and that need to be displayed on multiple pages.

To update a library item:

1   In the Assets panel, select the Library category and then select the item you want to update.
2   Click the Edit button at the bottom of the panel. The item opens in a separate window.
3   Edit the item and save the file. The Update Library Items dialog box opens.
4   Click Update. The Update Pages dialog box opens.
5   Click Close, and then close the library file window.

Detaching library items

If you need to edit a specific instance of a library item, but you don't want to change the original library item, you can detach the instance. This severs the link to the original file, allowing you to edit the item independently. This process will also prevent the page item from being updated if the original library item is changed.

To detach a library item, first select the instance you want to detach; then, in the Property inspector, click "Detach from original." Click OK to close the warning box that appears. You can also right-click the instance you want to detach and choose Detach From Original.

A-2: Updating a library item

Here's how	Here's why
1 In the Assets panel, select **Spice shaker graphic**	
Click 📝	(The Edit button.) To open Spice shaker graphic.lbi.
2 Delete the spice shaker graphic from the page	(Select it and press Delete.) You'll swap the image with another image of a spice shaker.
3 Activate the Files panel	
Expand the images subfolder	
4 Drag **spice_bottle.gif** to the page	The Image Tag Accessibility Attributes dialog box appears.
In the Alternate text box, type **Spice shaker**, and click **OK**	
5 Save Spice shaker graphic.lbi	The Update Library Items dialog box opens.
Click **Update**	To open the Update Pages dialog box.
Click **Close**	To close the dialog box.
Close Spice shaker graphic.lbi	To return to the Recipes page. The page now uses the new graphic.
6 Switch to index.html	The library item has been updated automatically on both pages.
Ask a student volunteer and facilitate a brief discussion. 7 How might this feature be useful to you in your own site projects?	*Answers will vary. If students have resources that often change and that need to be displayed on multiple pages, using the Library feature can save maintenance time, much in the same way that style sheets make it easier to update the formatting of a Web site.*

Snippets

Explanation

Another way that you can add repeating elements to your pages is to use the Snippets panel, shown in Exhibit 2-2. *Snippets* are sections of code that you can store and retrieve whenever you need them. Even if you're experienced with HTML, there are other languages, such as JavaScript or ActionScript, that you might need to draw on as you work on a site. Using the Snippets panel can save you time because you can store

ACA objective 2.1b

frequently used code blocks and scripts and then add them as needed, instead of typing the code by hand each time or repeatedly copying and pasting it from an external file. Using snippets also helps you maintain consistency and prevent errors and typos.

Exhibit 2-2: The Snippets panel

To open the Snippets panel, choose Window, Snippets. To create a snippet, select the code you want to use and then click the New Snippet button at the bottom of the Snippets panel. In the dialog box that appears, you can name the snippet, add a description, and select options to specify how you want to add the snippet to other site pages.

To add a snippet to a page, drag it from the Snippets panel onto the page, at the desired location. You can also place the insertion point where you want the snippet to go, and then double-click the snippet in the Snippets panel or click the Insert button. You can add snippets in both Design view and Code view.

Do it! ### A-3: Creating and inserting a snippet

Here's how	Here's why
1 In index.html, switch to Code view	You'll create and apply a code snippet.
2 Choose **Window, Snippets**	To open the Snippets panel.
At the bottom of the Snippets panel, click 🗁	To create a new Snippets folder.
Name the new folder **Outlander Header**	
3 Scroll to the top of the code	

Tell students that it's best to drag on the line numbers.

Select the entire masthead section, as shown	

Drag on the line numbers to select all the code on these lines.

ACA objective 2.1b

4 Click 🔁	(The New Snippet button is at the bottom of the Snippets panel.) To open the Snippet dialog box.
In the Name box, type **Header**	To give the snippet a name that indicates what it contains or how it's used.
In the Description box, enter **Outlander logo and navigation bar**	
5 Verify that **Wrap selection** is selected	
Next to Preview type, select **Design**	To show the logo and navbar, instead of the code, in the snippet preview.
Click **OK**	To close the dialog box and add the snippet.
Observe the Snippets panel	The snippet file is displayed in the new folder, and the preview shows the links in the header.

Be sure students select <none> in the Layout column.

6 Create a new, blank page	(Choose File, New. Under Page Type, select HTML. Under Layout, select none, and click Create.) You'll insert the snippet to get started on the new page.
Save the page as **new.html**	

7	Insert a line within the `<body>` section, as shown	``` 8 <body> 9 10 </body> ```
8	In the Snippets panel, double-click **Header**	The snippet is added to the code.
	Switch to Design view	The link content is there, but the logo isn't, and the navigation bar isn't formatted. This occurred because the page is not yet linked to a style sheet, which controls that formatting.
9	Activate the CSS Styles panel	If necessary.
10	Click [icon]	(The Attach Style Sheet button.) To open the Attach External Style Sheet dialog box.
	Click **Browse**	The Select Style Sheet File dialog box appears.
	Open the **styles** folder	In the Outlander folder.
	Select **globalstyle.css** and click **OK**	To select the style sheet and return to the Attach External Style Sheet dialog box.
	Click **OK**	The logo and background image appear, and the navigation bar is formatted.
11	Save and close new.html	

Tell students to click Update and then Close if they are asked to update library items.

Server-side includes

Explanation

A *server-side include* is a file that a Web server incorporates into your Web page when a browser requests that page from the server. Server-side includes are similar to library items, except that they're maintained by the server after you upload your site. They provide an efficient way to update pages without your having to make the changes manually and then re-upload the pages.

Advantages

ACA objective 2.1b

If you often need to change certain types of information, such as copyright statements, event listings, or news items, you can use server-side includes to simplify the process. You create and upload one file (the server-side include), and the server will automatically replace the content in any pages that reference it. This technique helps you maintain consistency across your site.

In general, server-side includes are a good way to update site pages when:

- Your site requires frequent editing.
- Your site is large.
- Two or more people manage the site from different locations.
- A client is updating the site and doesn't have Dreamweaver to take advantage of library items. (However, clients would need to understand how to update the content in the server-side include file and how to upload the file to the server.)

Before you decide to incorporate server-side includes in your site, you might need to check with your IT manager or service provider to ensure that server-side includes are supported, and determine what naming conventions are required. Some servers are configured to examine all files to see if they have server-side includes, whereas other servers search only for files with the .shtml (or .shtm) extension.

Creating server-side includes

To create a server-side include:

1 Open the document that contains the content you want to use for the server-side include.
2 In Code view, select the content you want to include. (Making the selection in Code view helps ensure that you're selecting all the code and content you want to include.)
3 Choose Edit, Copy (or press Ctrl+C).
4 Create a new, blank HTML document.
5 In Code view, select all of the code and press Delete.
6 Choose Edit, Paste (or press Ctrl+V).
7 Save the file as an HTML document. (If your service provider requires the .shtml or .shtm extension, save your file with that extension instead.)

Do it!

A-4:   Creating a server-side include

Here's how	Here's why
1 In index.html, scroll down to view the copyright statement	The copyright statement appears on every page. You'll create a server-side include to make updating the copyright statement easier, should it be necessary after the site is uploaded to the server.
Click in the copyright text	To place the insertion point.
2 Switch to Code view	If necessary.
Select the copyright code and the comments around it, as shown	
Press CTRL + C	To copy the code.
3 Create a new, blank HTML document	Because you were in Code view previously, the new document opens in Code view.
4 Press CTRL + A	To select all of the default page code.
Press DELETE	
5 Press CTRL + V	To paste the copyright code and content.
6 Save the file as **copyright.shtml**	To create the server-side include.
7 Close the file	

ACA objective 2.1b

Point out the file extension.

Code view panel contents:

```
54
55    <!-- Begin copyright secti
56       <div id="copyright">All co
57   <!-- End copyright section -->
58
```

Inserting server-side includes

Explanation

After you've created a server-side include, you can reference it in any of your site pages. When a user requests a page that contains a server-side include, the server processes the server-side include and replaces it with the content of the include file.

To insert a server-side include in a page:

1   Open the page on which you want to add the server-side include.
2   In Code view or Design view, place the cursor where you want to add the server-side include.
3   In the Insert panel, click the Server-Side Include button. (You can also choose Insert, Server-Side Include.) The Select File dialog box opens.
4   Navigate to the server-side include file and select it.
5   Click OK.

Although you can preview server-side includes in Design view, they won't appear if you preview your pages locally in a browser, because they require a server to process them.

Do it!

A-5:   Adding a server-side include

Here's how	Here's why
1 In index.html, verify that the copyright code is still selected	
2 Press (DELETE)	To delete the copyright statement. You'll replace it with the server-side include.
3 Scroll down in the Insert panel	
Click	(The Server-Side Include button.) The Select File dialog box appears.
Double-click **copyright.shtml**	To insert the server-side include.
Observe the code	Dreamweaver inserts a special code, which is processed by the server and replaced by the content in the include file.
4 Switch to Design view and verify the results	The copyright statement appears normally.
5 Click the copyright text	To select the server-side include.
Observe the Property inspector	The Property inspector shows attributes for the server-side include.
6 Save the page	You'll add the server-side include to another document.
7 In recipes.html, switch to Code view	
Scroll to the bottom	

⚠ If the copyright div isn't selected, tell students to select it first and then press Delete.

ACA objective 2.1b

8   Click to place the insertion point
    above the closing `</body>` tag

```
126        <!-- End conte
127
128
129     |
130
131        </body>
132        </html>
```

9   Choose **Insert**,
    Server-Side Include

    Select **copyright.shtml** and
    click **OK**

The Select File dialog box appears.

10 Switch to Design view

The copyright statement is now at the bottom of
the page.

11 Save the page

Updating server-side includes

Explanation

To update a server-side include, open the server-side include document, make the
required changes, and save it. When you upload the server-side include file to the
server, the changes will automatically be applied on every page that references it.

Do it!

A-6:   Editing a server-side include

Here's how	Here's why
1 In the recipes page, double-click the copyright statement	To open the copyright.shtml file.
Change 2008 to **2012**	
2 Save and close the file	
3 In recipes.html, verify the results	The copyright text has been updated to reflect the change in the include file.
4 Switch to index.html in Design view	The copyright statement has been updated universally. If the site were uploaded to a server, you'd need to re-upload only the server-side include file for the changes to be made throughout the site.
5 Save and close all open documents	

Topic B: Templates

This topic covers the following Adobe ACA exam objectives for Dreamweaver CS5.

#	Objective
2.1b	Identify techniques used to maintain consistency.
5.5a	Demonstrate knowledge of Dreamweaver templates.
5.5b	Demonstrate knowledge of how to create a new Dreamweaver template.
5.5c	Demonstrate knowledge of how to save an existing HTML file as a Dreamweaver template.
5.5d	Demonstrate knowledge of how to create and edit editable regions in a template.
5.5e	Demonstrate knowledge of how to apply or build pages from templates, and how to detach a template from a page.

Working with templates

Explanation

If you have multiple pages that share a common layout and/or common page elements, a template can help you develop and update those pages faster and more efficiently. With a template, you can design a layout that contains permanent, or fixed, page elements, and specify areas of a page that can be edited. You can then apply that template to multiple pages, changing the content in the editable areas while maintaining the content in the fixed areas.

ACA objective 5.5a

Templates can be especially useful if you're working with a team of people to develop a site. For example, one developer might create the overall design, with editable regions designated for content unique to each page. Other developers could then be responsible for adding page-specific content but wouldn't be able to modify the fixed regions established by the designer.

ACA objective 2.1b

Templates can also help you maintain consistency across your site pages and make site maintenance faster and easier. If you need to change fixed areas of a template, changing them in the template applies the changes to all pages that are based on the template.

Creating templates

ACA objectives 5.5b, 5.5c

You can start with a new, blank template or create a template from an existing page. To create a blank template, choose File, New. Then select Blank Template, select a template from the Template Type list, and click Create.

To create a template from a page:

1 Create or open the page that you want to use as a template.
2 Choose File, Save as Template to open the Save as Template dialog box.
3 From the Site list, select the site in which you want to save the template.
4 In the Save as box, enter a unique name for the template. Click Save.

ACA objective 5.5d

Creating editable regions

Every template needs to contain at least one editable region for page-specific content. To create an editable region in a template:

1   Select the content that you want to set as an editable region, or place the insertion point where you want to create the editable region.

2   Choose Insert, Template Objects, Editable Region to open the Editable Region dialog box.

3   In the Name box, enter a unique name for the editable region. Click OK.

B-1: Creating a template

Here's how	Here's why
1 Choose **Site**, **New Site...**	To open the Site Setup dialog box.
2 In the Site Name box, type **Outlander templates**	To name the site.
3 Browse to the current topic folder	Student Data folder Unit 2\Topic B.
Open the Outlander folder, click **Select**, and then click **Save**	To set the root folder for this site and create the site.
4 Open aboutus.html	(From the Files panel.) You'll create a template from a Web page.
5 Choose **File**, **Save as Template...**	To open the Save As Template dialog box.
Edit the Save as box to read **Outlander**	
In the Description box, enter **Standard page layout**	To add a description to the template.
Click **Save**	A dialog box appears, asking if you'd like to update links.
6 Click **Yes**	To update the links. The file is saved as a DWT (Dreamweaver Template) file.
7 Observe the Files panel	Dreamweaver creates a folder named Templates for storing template files.
Expand the Templates folder, as shown	

ACA objectives 5.5a, 5.5b, 5.5c

⚠ *Be sure that students choose Save as Template, not Save As.*

```
Local Files
  ⊞ 📁 styles
  ⊟ 📁 Templates
         📄 Outlander.dwt
     📄 aboutus.html
```

To see that the new template document is saved in the Templates folder.

8 In the template, click in the first paragraph	To place the insertion point. You'll delete this section and replace it with an editable region.
Press `CTRL` + `A`	To select everything in the `<div>` tag.
Type **Page Content**	
	This will serve as placeholder text for the editable region. Using placeholder text in your templates will help you distinguish editable regions from locked regions.
9 Triple-click **Page content**	To select the text. You want the text to be editable, not the container it's in.

ACA objectives 2.1b, 5.5d

10 Choose **Insert**, **Template Objects**, **Editable Region**	To open the New Editable Region dialog box.
Edit the Name box to read **MainContent** and click **OK**	
	The area is marked as an editable region, and the name appears as a label.
11 Save the template	You'll continue to work on this template in the next activity.

Tell students that they should name editable regions descriptively to make it easier for other developers to understand the purpose of each region.

Editable attributes

Explanation

You can set a template to allow users to edit the attributes of certain elements. For example, you can allow template users to change the value of a `class` or `id` attribute to take advantage of style options in a style sheet.

When you create an editable tag attribute, Dreamweaver inserts a variable in the template code. The default, or initial, value is set in the template, and users can then change the value as needed in their template-based documents.

To create an editable attribute:

1. Select the element for which you want to create an editable attribute.
2. Choose Modify, Templates, Make Attribute Editable.
3. In the Editable Tag Attributes dialog box, select an attribute from the Attribute list, or click Add to enter an attribute name manually.
4. If you click Add to specify an attribute, a dialog box opens. Type a valid attribute name, such as `class` or `id`, and click OK.
5. Verify that "Make attribute editable" is selected.
6. In the Label box, enter a descriptive name for the attribute.
7. From the Type list, select the type of value that will be allowed. For most situations in which you're enabling the editing of HTML attributes, you should choose Text.
8. In the Default box, enter the initial value for the attribute. If you're using a `class` or `id` attribute to enable style modifications, you can make the default value an actual class name in the style sheet, or use a "dummy" `class` or `id` name if the initial value is not meant to affect the formatting.
9. Click OK.

Do it!   **B-2:   Creating an editable attribute**

In this activity, students will set up the template to allow template users to apply a different background color to the content area by using a class that's already in the style sheet.

Here's how	Here's why
1 Click in the editable region	To place the insertion point.
In the Tag selector, click **<div#content>**	You'll create an editable attribute for this element.
2 Choose **Modify**, **Templates**, **Make Attribute Editable...**	To open the Editable Tag Attributes dialog box.
3 Click [Add...]	
Type **class** and click **OK**	You'll allow users to modify the value of the class attribute so they can take advantage of a rule in the style sheet.
4 In the Label box, type **class**	This label will serve as a prompt for the template user.
From the Type list, select **Text**	(If necessary.) The value entered by the template user will be text, instead of a number, a Boolean value (true/false), or a URL.
In the Default box, type **normal**	This will indicate to the template user that the default value will have no effect. The template user will need to be aware of the class names in the style sheet to take advantage of this feature.
5 Click **OK**	
6 Save and close the template	You'll change the value of this attribute in the next activity.

Creating pages from a template

Explanation

You can create new pages from a template, or you can apply a template to existing pages. When you apply a template to a page that already has content, you need to assign the content to the template's editable regions. However, when you create a new page (with no content other than the fixed content of the template), there's no need to match that content to the template's editable regions.

ACA objective 2.1b

Creating pages from a template can save a lot of time because you don't have to re-enter any common elements on each page. It also guarantees consistency across your site pages.

ACA objective 5.5e

To create a page from a template:

1 Choose File, New to open the New Document dialog box.
2 In the list on the left, select Page from Template.
3 In the Site list, select the site that includes the template. (The current site will be selected by default.)
4 From the Template list, select the template you want to use.
5 Click Create.

Detaching a page from a template

ACA objective 5.5e

If you're working on a page that's attached to a template and you need to modify something that is not in an editable region, you must first detach the page from the template. To detach do so, choose Modify, Templates, Detach from Template. This makes the entire page editable and strips out all the template code.

Do it!

B-3: Applying a template and a template attribute

Here's how	Here's why
1 Choose **File, New...**	You'll create a Web page based on the template you created.
2 On the left side of the dialog box, select **Page from Template**	
Verify that the **Outlander** template is selected	A preview of the template is displayed.
3 Verify that **Update page when template changes** is checked	
ACA objectives 2.1b, 5.5e Click **Create**	To create a new, untitled page based on the Outlander template.
4 Save the page as **books.html**	

5 Point to an empty area of the page	
	The pointer changes to indicate that you can't edit this area of the page. Only areas designated as editable regions can be modified.
6 Observe the top-right corner of the Document window	Dreamweaver creates a label to indicate that the page is based on the Outlander template.
7 Triple-click **Page Content**	To select the placeholder text. You'll delete it and replace it with content from another file.
Press (DELETE)	
8 Open Books.txt	From the Files panel.
Press (CTRL) + (A)	To select all the content in the file.
Press (CTRL) + (C)	To copy the content.
Close Books.txt	Don't save changes.
9 Click inside the editable region	To place the insertion point.
Press (CTRL) + (V)	To paste the content into the editable region.
10 Choose **Modify, Template Properties...**	To open the Template Properties dialog box. You'll change the template variable that you made editable.
Observe the dialog box	The variable is `class`, and the initial value is `normal`. The label you created earlier creates the prompt for you to change the value of the `class` attribute for this Div section.
Edit the class box to read **highlight**	The style sheet has a class style named "highlight," which applies a pale green background color.
Click **OK**	To change the template variable. The editable region now appears with a green background.
11 Save and close the document	In the next activity, you'll apply the Outlander template to a page that already has content.

Applying a template to a page that already has content

Explanation

When you apply a template to a page that already has content, you need to specify where that content should be placed within the template. When you apply a template to an existing page, Dreamweaver displays the Inconsistent Region Names dialog box, shown in Exhibit 2-3, so that you can match the content with the template's editable regions.

To apply a template to a page that has content:

1 Open the page to which you want to apply the template.

2 In the Assets panel, click the Templates button to display the available templates.

ACA objective 5.5e

3 From the Templates list, drag the desired template onto the page. The Inconsistent Region Names dialog box opens.

4 Select the content you want to apply to a region.

5 From the "Move content to new region" list, select the region you want to use for the selected content.

6 Repeat steps 4 and 5 for the remaining page content.

7 Click OK.

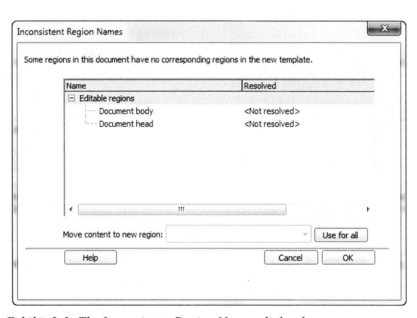

Exhibit 2-3: The Inconsistent Region Names dialog box

Do it!

B-4:   Applying a template to an existing page

Here's how	Here's why
1 Open products.html	(From the Files panel.) This page contains a table with spice descriptions.
2 Activate the Assets panel	
3 Click 🗐	(The Templates button.) To display the templates in the current site.
Click ↻	To refresh the list. The Outlander template is the only available template.
ACA objective 5.5e 4 Drag the Outlander template onto the page	The Inconsistent Region Names dialog box opens.
5 Select **Document body**	
From the "Move content to new region" list, select **MainContent**	To move the existing content into the template's editable region.
Select **Document head**	
From the "Move content to new region" list, select **head**	To move the page's <head> content into the template's <head> section. This prevents you from creating a duplicate <head> section.
Click **OK**	The template is successfully applied to the page.
6 Save and close the document	

Topic C: Head elements

This topic covers the following Adobe ACA exam objectives for Dreamweaver CS5.

#	Objective
3.2b	Demonstrate knowledge of how to change between the categories on the Insert bar.
5.7a	Demonstrate knowledge of head content, meta tags, and the Tag selector.
5.7b	Demonstrate knowledge of how to add and edit head content by using the Common category on the Insert bar.

Working with head elements

Explanation

The `<head>` section of a Web page contains resources for and information about the current document, such as a page title, keywords, scripts, internal style sheet rules, or a link to an external style sheet. The contents of a document's `<head>` section are never displayed in the browser.

You can enter head content directly in Code view, or you can use the Property inspector to enter and edit head content. The following table describes elements commonly used inside the `<head>` section of a document.

ACA objective 5.7a

Item	Description
Meta tags	*Meta tags* provide information about the current document. For example, the `<keywords>` meta tag lists words that are relevant to the page's content and are used by some search engines to help users find information. Similarly, the `<description>` meta tag is used by some search engines to categorize and summarize your site. Meta tags can also specify page properties, such as character encoding, the author, or copyright information.
Title	The `<title>` tag holds the text that appears in the browser's title bar. Search engines refer to a Web page by its title.
Scripts	Scripts (usually JavaScript) may appear in the `<head>` section of pages that have dynamic content or functionality.
Reference links	The `<head>` section can include links to files, such as external style sheets and scripts.
Style	The `<style>` section holds the CSS styles that constitute a page's internal style sheet.

Descriptions and keywords

Providing a description of your site or of individual pages, as well as providing keywords, can be important to the site's effectiveness with some search engines. When a search engine user submits search terms, search engines return a list of sites, usually listed according to the best match. Writing effective keywords and a page or site description can help improve your ranking in some search engines.

Descriptions can improve the overall quality of the search result. For example, Google and Yahoo use a site's description as the text that appears below a Web site's link in many search results. If a description isn't present, some search engines use the first text they encounter on the page, and this text might not provide the first impression you want to make.

Because visitors often enter a site through its home page, it's common practice to provide a description and a list of keywords on the index (home) page. However, you can list keywords and descriptions for as many pages as you like.

Do it!

C-1: Discussing head elements

Facilitate a brief discussion for each question.

ACA objective 5.7a

Questions	Answers
1 Which elements might you want to include in the `<head>` section of your home page?	• *Meta tags* • *Title* • *JavaScript or a link to an external script* • *Internal CSS rules or a link to a style sheet*
2 What are some benefits of using meta tags?	• *They allow you to provide information about the Web site, its authors, or specific pages. This information doesn't appear in a browser.* • *They can result in more accurate and efficient search engine matches.* • *Many search engines display the text in a Description meta tag under the link to the page in the search results.*
3 How can `<keyword>` meta tags help drive more traffic to your site?	*Some search engines use keywords to create matches with users' search criteria. The more accurate your keywords are in relation to the content or services you provide, the more likely it is that your Web site will rank high in relevant searches.*
4 Where does the text in a `<title>` element appear?	*Page titles appear in the browser's title bar, at the top of the application window.*

Meta tag icons

Explanation

There are more than 30 types of meta tags. You can display a document's head elements as a series of icons at the top of the Document window, as shown in Exhibit 2-4. When you click one of these icons, the corresponding element's attributes appear in the Property inspector. To display a page's head content as a series of icons, choose View, Head Content or press Ctrl+Shift+H.

Exhibit 2-4: The Meta, Title, and Link icons in the Document window

Do it!

C-2: Exploring head elements

The files for this activity are in Student Data folder **Unit 2\Topic C**.

Here's how	Here's why
1 Choose **File**, **Open**	
Browse to the current topic folder	
In the Outlander folder, open index.html	You'll examine the elements in the `<head>` section.
2 Choose **View**, **Head Content**	To display the `<head>` section icons at the top of the Document window.
3 Click	(The Meta icon.) To display the meta data in the document.
Observe the Property inspector	This page uses ISO-8859-1 character set encoding, which is a character set typically used in sites with languages that use a Latin alphabet, such as English. Dreamweaver writes this tag into the page by default.
4 Click	(The Title icon.) To display the page title.
Observe the Property inspector	The title of this Web page is "Outlander Spices."
5 Click	(The Link icon.) To display the style sheet linked to this page.
Observe the Property inspector	This page is linked to a style sheet named globalstyle.css. If the `<head>` section had multiple link resources, a separate icon would be displayed for each one.

Tell students they don't need to define a site for this activity.

ACA objective 5.7a

Tell students that this encoding information is important because some applications and search engines use it to provide language-specific search results.

Students will change this title in the next activity.

Editing head elements

Explanation

Dreamweaver makes it easy to edit the content in your meta tags. Click the icon for the head element you want to edit, and then make the desired content changes in the Property inspector. Exhibit 2-5 shows the Property inspector when the Title icon is selected.

Exhibit 2-5: A document title in the Property inspector

Using the Insert panel to add head content

ACA objectives 3.2b, 5.7b

You can insert head content by using the Insert panel (or the Insert bar, depending on your workspace layout). Select the Common category; then scroll down and click Head to display the Head content list. Select an option from the list to open a dialog box specific to the selected type of content. After you have selected an option, the Head button changes to show the last content type that was selected. To display the list again to select a different type of head content, click the small arrow.

Do it!

C-3: Editing a head element

Here's how	Here's why
1 Click the Title icon	You'll change the page title.
2 In the Property inspector, edit the Title box to read **Outlander Spices: Welcome!**	
3 Switch to Code view	The `<title>` tag and the new title are highlighted.
Return to Design view	
Save the page	
4 Preview the page in Internet Explorer	Press F12.
Verify that the new title appears in the browser's title bar	
Close the browser	

Keywords

Explanation

As mentioned earlier, it's important to specify keywords relevant to a page or site because some search engines use these keywords to help provide accurate search results.

Scan your pages and create a list of words that are relevant to your site's purpose and content. Include words that might not appear in your site's content but are likely to be entered by a user. For example, the word "seasonings" doesn't appear in the Outlander Spices Web site, but the word is relevant to the site and it's a word that users might enter in a search engine.

To enter your keywords:

1   Choose Insert, HTML, Head Tags, Keywords.
2   In the Keywords dialog box, type a list of keywords, separated by commas.
3   Click OK.

Do it!

C-4:   Defining keywords for your site

ACA objective 5.7a

Here's how	Here's why
1 Choose **Insert**, **HTML**, **Head Tags**, **Keywords**	To open the Keywords dialog box.
2 In the Keywords box, enter **spices, outlander, cooking, seasonings, ingredients**	To create a list of relevant keywords that users are likely to enter in a search engine.
Click **OK**	To add the keywords.
3 Observe the `<head>` section of the Document window	A Keywords icon is displayed.
4 Click the Keywords icon	
Observe the Property inspector	The keywords appear in the Keywords box. You can make further changes in the keywords list in the Property inspector.
5 Save the page	

⚠ *Be sure that students separate keywords with commas.*

Tell students that the Keywords icon might appear elsewhere in the sequence of icons.

Descriptions

Explanation

Your site description should be a concise statement that describes the purpose or content of your site (or a specific page in the site). Most search engine users are looking for the best results as quickly as possible. Users might skip over a long or poorly written description. Also, the search engine might display only the first line or two of the description.

To insert a description, choose Insert, HTML, Head Tags, Description. Enter your description in the Description dialog box, and click OK.

Do it!

ACA objective 5.7a

C-5:   Creating a description of your site

Here's how	Here's why
1 Choose **Insert**, **HTML**, **Head Tags**, **Description**	To open the Description dialog box. You'll add a description that a search engine might use to index your site and might display on a search results page.
2 In the Description box, enter **Outlander Spices provides quality spices for cooking and baking of all kinds.** Click **OK**	
3 Observe the `<head>` section of the Document window	A Description icon appears
4 Observe the Property inspector	The description appears in the Description box.
5 Switch to Code view Return to Design view	The meta tag you created is highlighted. The name of the tag is `<description>`, and the tag's content is the actual description text.
Facilitate a brief discussion. 6 Why is it important to write a concise statement as your site description?	*Some search engines use descriptions in their list of search results. This text could provide a first impression of your site, and the clearer and more relevant it is, the more likely it is to help users find what they're looking for and increase your site's traffic.*
7 Save and close index.html	

Topic D: Images and multimedia

This topic covers the following Adobe ACA exam objectives for Dreamweaver CS5.

#	Objective
1.5b	Identify page elements that are affected by end-user technical factors, such as download speed, screen resolution, operating system, and browser type.
4.4e	Demonstrate knowledge of using Photoshop Smart Objects.
4.6a	Demonstrate knowledge of best practices when incorporating Adobe Flash elements into a Web page.
4.6b	Demonstrate knowledge of how to add SWF and Flash video files to a Web page.
4.6c	Demonstrate knowledge of how to view SWF and Flash video files in Live mode.
5.4a	Demonstrate knowledge of the capabilities and limitations of editing or modifying images in Dreamweaver.
5.4b	Demonstrate knowledge of how to scale an image.
5.4c	Demonstrate knowledge of editing static and interactive assets with Fireworks, Photoshop, and Flash from inside Dreamweaver.

Working with multimedia files

Explanation

Dreamweaver makes it easy to add sound, video, and Flash files to your Web pages so that you can deliver content in ways that static text alone can't.

Flash content

ACA objectives 1.5b, 4.6a

You can insert Flash content in SWF or FLV format. If you insert a SWF file and it contains an embedded video, the file will have to download completely before a user can begin to view the video content. For this reason, SWF is best when the video has a small file size and short duration.

After you insert a SWF file, you can use the Property inspector to set its height and width on the page, adjust the video quality, set the animation to play automatically when the page loads, set it to play in a continuous loop, and apply styles to it.

To insert a SWF file:

ACA objective 4.6b

1   Place the insertion point on the page and do either of the following:
    - Choose Insert, Media, SWF.
    - On the Common tab in the Insert panel, click the Media button and select SWF. (If the button already reads Media:SWF, you can click it or drag it to the page.)
2   In the Select SWF dialog box, select a SWF file and click OK. A SWF placeholder is displayed on the page.
3   In the Property inspector, edit the file properties as needed.

When you save the page, a message appears, stating that two dependent files were created and saved in a Scripts folder in the site. These files are required for the Flash content to work, so it's critical that you upload the Scripts folder along with your other site files and folders.

ACA objective 4.6c

After you have inserted a SWF file, you can view it by using Dreamweaver's Live view. First, though, you'll need to install the Flash Plug-in, using the Firefox browser, and then restart your computer.

Inserting FLV files

ACA objectives 1.5b, 4.6a

If you want to deliver Flash video (FLV files), you can choose streaming video or progressive downloading. If you want to deliver streaming video, you need a server running the Flash Media Server platform. When you stream video, the user doesn't have to wait until the entire file is downloaded. Streaming allows you to determine the bandwidth limitations of site visitors and deliver content accordingly. You can also provide additional interactivity, such as user controls, along with the video content.

If you deliver FLV content via progressive downloading, you do not need Flash Media Server. Progressive downloading has many of the same benefits of streaming, except for the bandwidth detection capability

ACA objective 4.6b

To insert an FLV file:

1 Place the insertion point on the page and do either of the following:
   - Choose Insert, Media, FLV.
   - On the Common tab in the Insert panel, click the Media button and select FLV. (If the button already reads Media:FLV, you can click it or drag it to the page.)
2 In the Insert FLV dialog box, select either Progressive Download Video or Streaming Video.
3 Type the path to the FLV file in the URL box; or click Browse to open the Select FLV file dialog box, locate and select the FLV file, and click OK.
4 Set other properties as needed, and click OK.

Editing Flash content from within Dreamweaver

ACA objective 5.4c

You can integrate other Adobe products with Dreamweaver to streamline your development process and workflow. For example, if you have both Flash and Dreamweaver installed, you can select any SWF placeholder in Dreamweaver and then click Edit in the Property inspector to edit the object in Flash. You can also right-click the SWF placeholder and choose Edit with Flash.

Do it!

D-1: Inserting Flash content

The files for this activity are in Student Data folder **Unit 2\Topic D**.

Here's how	Here's why
1 Choose **Site, New Site...**	To open the Site Setup dialog box.
2 In the Site Name box, type **Outlander media**	To name the site.
3 Browse to the current topic folder	Student Data folder Unit 2\Topic D.
Open the Outlander folder, click **Select**, and then click **Save**	To set the root folder for the site and create the site.
4 Open cookbook.html	From the Files panel.
5 Click above the first paragraph	

You'll embed a SWF file here.

6 In the Insert panel, select the **Common** category	If necessary.

Tell students to scroll down in the Insert panel, if necessary.

Click	The Media button.
Select **SWF**	The Select SWF dialog box opens.
7 Open the media subfolder	

ACA objectives 4.6a, 4.6b

Select **bookpromo.swf** and click **OK**	The Object Tag Accessibility Attributes dialog box appears.
8 In the Title box, enter **Outlander cookbook feature (Flash)**	To specify Alt text for users with screen readers and other assistive devices. When you embed media, it's important to indicate the file type in your Alt text.
Click **OK**	A Flash placeholder appears on the page.
9 In the Property inspector, click **Play**	To preview the Flash file.
Click **Stop**	In the Property inspector.

10 Save your changes

    Click **OK**   To copy the dependent files.

If necessary, have students click the Refresh button in the Files panel.

11 Observe the Files panel   Dreamweaver automatically created a Scripts folder to store the video's dependent files.

12 Close cookbook.html

Windows Media Player movies

Explanation

In addition to SWF and FLV files, you can deliver Windows Media Player movies, QuickTime movies, and other media objects. Windows Media Player is a popular video format for delivering multimedia content. WMF files provide the user with a set of playback controls.

To insert a Windows Media Player file:

1   Place the insertion point on the page.
2   In the Common category of the Insert panel, click the Media button and select Plugin. (If the button already reads Media:Plugin, you can click it or drag it to the page.) The Select File dialog box opens.
3   Select a WMV file and click OK.
4   In the Property inspector, edit the file's properties as needed.

Media file sizing

Many media file types, including Windows Media Player and QuickTime, provide playback controls for the user. The developer of the movie file should provide you with the optimum viewing dimensions for the movie file, in pixels. For Windows Media files, you might need to add 64 pixels to the height to accommodate the playback controls at the bottom of the movie object. For QuickTime movies, you might need to add 20 pixels to accommodate its playback controls.

Do it!

D-2:   Inserting a Windows Media Player file

The files for this activity are in Student Data folder **Unit 2\Topic D**.

Here's how	Here's why
1 Open video.html	
2 Click below the heading	(Below "Cooking with Outlander.") You'll insert a Windows Media Player movie here.
3 Choose **Insert**, **Media**, **Plugin**	The Select File dialog box opens.
In the media folder, select **cookingvideo.wmv**	
Click **OK**	
4 In the Property inspector, in the W box, enter **320**	To set the width of the video to 320 pixels.
5 Set the height to **304**	The actual height of the video is 240 pixels, but you need to add another 64 pixels to accommodate the user controls at the bottom of the movie.
6 Save the file and preview it in Internet Explorer	(Press F12.) To test the movie.
Point to the Windows Media Player controls	Tooltips describe the function of each control.
7 Click the Pause button	
Click the Play button	
When the movie ends, close the browser	
8 Close video.html	

Tell students they can also open the Media list in the Insert panel and select Plugin.

The WMV file might not be displayed properly in Live View, so be sure students open the page in their browsers.

If the movie doesn't start playing automatically, tell students to press Play.

Editing images

Explanation

You can perform basic image editing directly in Dreamweaver. For example, you can optimize, resize, crop, and sharpen an image, or adjust its brightness and contrast. You don't need to have Photoshop or Fireworks installed to make these types of edits.

ACA objectives 5.4a, 5.4b

To edit an image, select it in the Document window and choose Modify, Image. A menu of basic editing options is displayed. The Optimize, Brightness/Contrast, and Sharpen commands open dialog boxes you can use to adjust the corresponding settings. These image editing features work only with JPEG and GIF images, and they do not offer the same level of control and precision that specialized programs like Photoshop and Fireworks provide. However, when you only need to make basic changes, Dreamweaver's image editing options are effective.

Resizing and resampling

You can select an image and drag its resize handles to change its dimensions. You can also use the W and H boxes in the Property inspector to enter specific width and height values in pixels. When you resize an image with either method, the image might look distorted until you resample it. Resampling smoothes the edges of a resized image and can reduce its file size for faster downloading.

Photoshop Smart Objects

ACA objective 4.4e

If you also work with Photoshop, you can integrate Photoshop files into Dreamweaver by using Smart Objects. A Photoshop *Smart Object* is an image that contains a link to a Photoshop file (a .PSD file). You don't need to open Photoshop to change a Smart Object in Dreamweaver. When you edit a Smart Object in Dreamweaver, the original Photoshop file remains unchanged. If changes are made in the original PSD file, you can select the image in Design view (in Dreamweaver) and click Update from Original (in the Property inspector) to synchronize the image with the Photoshop asset. A Smart Object is identified by an icon in the image's upper-left corner.

Do it!

ACA objectives 5.4a, 5.4b

D-3: Editing an image

The files for this activity are in Student Data folder **Unit 2\Topic D**.

Here's how	Here's why
1 Open index.html	
2 Select the "Spice of the Month" image	(On the left side of the page.) Three black squares (resize handles) are displayed.
Edit the W box to read **160**	(In the Property inspector.) To reduce the width of the image.
3 Observe the text in the image	The image appears slightly distorted after it's resized.
4 Choose **Modify**, **Image**, **Resample**	A message appears.
Click **OK**	To resample the image.
5 Observe the text in the image	It no longer looks distorted.
6 Choose **Modify**, **Image**, **Brightness/Contrast**	To open the Brightness/Contrast dialog box.
Drag the Contrast slider until the box reads **10**	To increase the color contrast in the image.
Click **OK**	
7 Save and close index.html	

Unit summary: Site assets

Topic A

In this topic, you learned how to create **library items** and add them to a page. You learned how to update a library item, and update multiple pages by changing a library item used on those pages. You learned how to create and use code **snippets**, and you learned how to create a **server-side include** file and reference it in your site pages. You also learned how to edit a server-side include to update all site pages that refer to it.

Topic B

In this topic, you learned how to create and apply **templates**. You learned how to define **editable regions** and **editable attributes**, and you learned how to create new pages from a template. Finally, you learned how to apply a template to pages that already have content.

Topic C

In this unit, you learned about common **<head> elements**. You learned how to edit <head> elements and add **keywords** and a **site description** to potentially improve search engine results.

Topic D

In this topic, you learned how to add **media files** to your pages. You inserted **Flash** content, and you learned about the difference between delivering SWF files and FLV files, along with the requirements for streaming video. You also learned how to insert **Windows Media Player** files and **edit images** directly in Dreamweaver.

Independent practice activity

In this activity, you'll create a library item and add it to a page. Then you'll save the page as a template, add keywords and a description to the page, create a page from the template, and add a SWF file to a page.

The files for this activity are in Student Data folder **Unit 2\Unit summary**.

1 Create a site named **Assets practice**, using the Outlander folder as the local root folder. (The Outlander folder is in the Unit summary folder.)

2 Open recipes.html.

3 Create a library item named **recipeDisclaimer** that includes the following text: **When trying any new recipe, sample the results periodically and adjust the amount of spice to taste.**

4 Add the new library item to recipes.html. Place it between the recipe and the copyright footer. (*Hint:* Drag the library item to the <div> tag above the copyright section.)

5 Apply the class style **disclaimer** to the text.

6 Save recipes.html as a template named **recipes**.

7 In the recipes template, make both columns editable regions. Then save and close the template.

8 Create a new page from the recipes.dwt template. Save the page with a name of your choice.

9 Delete the contents of the editable regions.

10 Save and close the page.

11 Open index.html.

12 View the document's <head> content.

13 Add the following keywords: **recipes**, **spices**, **outlander**.

14 Add a fitting description for the page, and save and close the file.

15 Open cookbook.html.

16 Click above the paragraph and insert the Flash file videopromo.swf. (The file is in the media folder.)

17 Save the page and preview it in Internet Explorer. Verify that the Flash file plays automatically when the page opens.

18 Save and close all open files.

Review questions

1 If you detach an instance of a library item and then edit the content on the page, the original library item:

  A Is deleted.

  B Is updated accordingly.

  C Is not affected.

  D Replaces the changed content the next time the page is opened.

2 If your site consists of hundreds of pages, and each page contains the same library item for a page footer, what happens if you edit the original library item?

  A When you open each page in Dreamweaver, a dialog box asks if you want the item to be updated.

  B All instances of the item are updated automatically.

  C Only the open document is updated.

  D You can't edit the original library item.

3 How can you place a server-side include on a page? [Choose all that apply.]

  A Place the insertion point where you want the server-side include and choose Insert, Server-Side Include.

  B Place the insertion point where you want the server-side include, and drag from the Link pickwhip in the Property inspector to the server-side include file in the Files panel.

  C Place the insertion point where you want the server-side include and click the Server-Side Include button in the Insert panel.

  D Right-click where you want the server-side include and choose Add Server-Side Include.

4 If you apply a template to a page with content that wasn't designed for that template, what happens?

  A You can't apply a template to a page that wasn't created for that template.

  B Dreamweaver applies the template automatically.

  C Dreamweaver prompts you to specify which regions of the page content should be applied to the template regions.

  D Dreamweaver prompts you to save the page as a new template file.

5 When you create an editable attribute in a template and set an initial value, what is the value of the attribute when a user creates a page based on the template?

A New pages based on the template retain the initial value of the template, and template users can apply new values.

B New pages based on the template will have the user's preference set as the default value.

C There is no initial value until the template user applies one manually.

D In new pages based on the template, users will not be able to modify the attribute.

6 How can you display a page's `<head>` content in Design view?

A Triple-click anywhere on the Document toolbar.

B Choose View, Head Content.

C Right-click the page and choose View Head Content.

D In the Property inspector, click Page Properties.

7 True or false? When you apply a template to a page that already has content, Dreamweaver automatically assigns the content to the largest editable region.

False. You need to specify where to place the content by using the Inconsistent Region Names dialog box, which opens when you apply a template to a page with content.

8 True or false? If a SWF file contains an embedded video, you can set it to stream so that users don't have to wait until the video has downloaded fully.

False. SWF files that contain an embedded video cannot be streamed. The SWF file will need to download completely before a user can begin viewing the video content.

9 Inserting SWF files with embedded video is best in which circumstance?

A When you want to deliver streaming video content.

B When you want to deliver streaming video content but do not have the Flash Media Server.

C When the video has a small file size and short duration.

D When you think your audience might not have the Flash video plug-in installed in their browsers.

10 True or false? When you insert a SWF file, Dreamweaver automatically creates a Scripts folder in the site folder and stores two dependent files in it.

True. When you publish your site, you need to be sure that you upload the Scripts folder; otherwise, browsers won't be able to display the SWF content properly.

Unit 3

Forms

Unit time: 75 minutes

Complete this unit, and you'll know how to:

A Create a form and add input fields, ensure form accessibility, set the tab order of input fields, and validate form data by using Spry widgets.

Topic A: Creating interactive forms

This topic covers the following Adobe ACA exam objectives for Dreamweaver CS5.

#	Objective
2.4a	List elements used to improve website usability.
3.1b	Demonstrate knowledge of the difference between Design view, Code view, Split view, and Live mode.
3.2a	Identify types of content that can be created or inserted by using the Insert bar.
3.2b	Demonstrate knowledge of how to change between the categories on the Insert bar.
4.11a	Demonstrate knowledge of which form inputs are appropriate for collecting various types of information.
4.11b	Demonstrate knowledge of how to use Dreamweaver to insert various form elements on a page.
4.11c	Demonstrate knowledge of methods used to transmit form data.

Web forms

Explanation

Web forms enable users to interact with your Web site. Typically, users fill out Web forms to create an account, make a purchase, provide user feedback, or request information. The information entered on the form is usually sent to a database. Dreamweaver provides several tools that make it easy to create and modify forms.

Form elements

In HTML, the `<form>` tag opens a form container. All form input fields must be placed inside this `<form>` container. When a user fills out the form and submits the information, the information is sent to a Web server for processing and storage in a database.

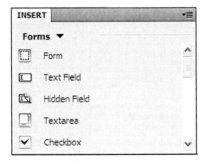

Exhibit 3-1: A form

To create a form, place the insertion point where you want the form to appear and click the Form button in the Forms category of the Insert panel. You can also drag the Form button to the desired location on the page.

Form input fields typically don't line up neatly on a page, but you can use a table to arrange form elements. For example, the form shown in Exhibit 3-1 is arranged in a table so that the input fields line up vertically.

Form tools

The Forms category in the Insert panel, shown in Exhibit 3-2, contains a button for each form element. Scroll through the list to find the form element you want to insert.

Exhibit 3-2: The Forms category of the Insert panel

The following table describes some of the most commonly used form object buttons.

Element	Button	Description
Form		Acts as a container to define the beginning and end of a form. To create a form, start with this element.
Text Field		Accepts a single word or short phrase, such as a name or address.
Textarea		Accepts longer text entries for such things as user feedback, support questions, or posts in a message board forum.
Checkbox		Allows a user to select an option. Typically used when multiple items can be selected.
Radio Button		Allows a user to select one item from a group of items.
Radio Group		Creates a group of related radio buttons, complete with labels and line breaks.
List/Menu		Displays a list from which the user can select one or more items.
Jump Menu		Inserts an object that is similar to a List/Menu, but each item in a jump menu is a hyperlink.
Image Field		Displays an image file in the form. The image can be used as a button.
File Field		Allows a user to browse to a file for uploading.
Button		Submits a completed form or clears all entries.
Label		Associates a text prompt with a form element by matching it with an ID. This association also enables a user to select a form element by clicking the text label, and this feature enhances usability.
Fieldset		Draws a box around a group of related form elements.
Hidden Field		Passes parameters to the Web server. These fields are "hidden" because they do not appear in the browser.

ACA objectives 3.2a, 4.11a

ACA objective 2.4a

Do it!   **A-1:   Starting a form**

The files for this activity are in Student Data folder **Unit 3\Topic A**.

Here's how	Here's why
1 Choose **Site, New Site...**	To open the Site Setup dialog box.
2 In the Site Name box, type **Outlander forms**	To name the site.
3 Browse to the current topic folder	Student Data folder Unit 3\Topic A.
Open the Outlander folder, click **Select**, and then click **Save**	To set the root folder for this site and create the site.
Tell students to make sure they are in Design view. 4 From the Files panel, open info.html	This page contains tables and text prompts that you'll use to build a form. Tables are commonly used to arrange form input fields.
5 Click in the space above the table, as shown	You'll insert a form container here.
6 In the Insert panel, click **Common**	
ACA objective 3.2b Select **Forms**	To display the form tools.
ACA objective 4.11b Click [ ]	(The Form button.) To insert a form at the insertion point. In Design view, Dreamweaver displays a dotted red box to indicate the form container.
7 Switch to Code view	To see the form code. Form-related code is orange to distinguish it from other code.
Tell students that in their real work, they'd link an action file, such as a CGI or JSP script, to the form to make it interface with a database. Locate the closing `</form>` tag	When you insert a form, the closing tag, `</form>`, is added directly after the opening tag. All form elements must be inside this form container, so you'll cut the closing tag and paste it at the bottom of the page.

8 Select the `</form>` tag

```
<form id="form1"
</form>
<br />
<table width="420
```

Press CTRL + X   To cut the tag.

Scroll to the bottom of the code

Point out that if students were starting a page from scratch, they would not have to move the closing <form> tag.

Directly below the CLOSE FORM comment, paste the tag

```
<!-- CLOSE FORM -->

</form>
```

Press Ctrl+V.

9 Scroll up and observe the `<label>` tags   The page already contains labels, which define the text prompts for each input field.

10 Switch to Design view

Scroll down   Notice that the form container, indicated by a dotted red line, contains both tables. In the next activity, you'll add input fields to the table rows.

11 Save the page

Text input fields

Explanation

To collect text on a form, you can use text fields and textarea fields. A *text field* collects a single line of text and is used for a short, alphanumeric entry, such as a name or address. A *textarea field* is used for a longer entry that can span multiple lines. Textarea fields can collect long strings of text and are typically used for such things as site or product feedback and message board posting.

To insert a text field or a textarea field, place the insertion point on the page. Then click the appropriate button in the Forms category of the Insert panel, or drag the button to a location on the page.

For a text field, you can control its width (the number of characters that can be displayed) and the number of characters that a user can enter. For a textarea field, you can control its width and height. The field's width is expressed as the number of characters, and the height is expressed as the number of lines. When the text exceeds the width of the field, it wraps to the next line.

You can convert a text field to a textarea field and vice versa, if you need to make changes as you develop a form. In the Property inspector, click Single line to convert a textarea field to a text field. Click Multi line to convert a text field to a textarea field.

Input field IDs and names

Every input field you create must be named so that the information a user enters is submitted to the server as a name/value pair. For example, if you name a text input field FirstName, and a user enters the name "Joe" and submits the form, the data FirstName="Joe" is submitted for processing. Input fields cannot contain spaces.

When you insert a text input field, the Input Tag Accessibility Attributes dialog box opens. In this dialog box, you can specify an ID for the input field. Dreamweaver automatically adds a name attribute with a value that matches the ID you specify. This attribute allows you to apply styles specifically to an input field, and it enhances accessibility when matched with a label.

If you don't want to specify an ID, you can name a field by selecting the field and entering a name in the Property inspector.

A-2: Inserting text input fields

Here's how	Here's why

ACA objectives 4.11a, 4.11b

Remind students that they're inserting the form elements into a table so that the fields are aligned.

1 Drag 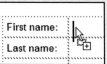 to the cell next to First name, as shown

(Drag the Text Field button from the Insert panel.) To insert a text input field. The Input Tag Accessibility Attributes dialog box opens.

There should be no space between the words

In the ID box, type **FirstName**

Specifying IDs for each input field allows you to associate the field with its label, and allows you to apply CSS styles to individual input fields.

Tell students that values entered in the Label box will appear as a label or text prompt for the input field on the page. On this page, labels are already set for each form element.

Select **No label tag**

This page already contains labels for each input field.

Click **OK**

2 Switch to Code view

Observe the input tag

When you specify an ID, Dreamweaver also adds the name attribute with a matching value. The name attribute creates the name/value pair, and the ID enhances the form's usability.

Switch to Design view

3 Drag 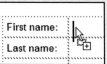 to the next row, next to the Last name prompt

In the ID box, type **LastName**

Attribute values cannot contain spaces, so using initial caps can help you read multiple-word values like this.

Verify that **No label tag** is selected

The form already contains labels for each text prompt. When you change a preference in this dialog box, it sticks until you change it again.

Click **OK**

Tell students to leave the cells next to the Gender and Country prompts empty and to use the prompts as a guide for their ID names.

4 Insert text fields for the other prompts in the first table

Leave the cells next to the Gender and Country prompts empty for now. Use the text prompts as a guide for your ID names.

5 Click the **First name** field

You'll change the width of this and other fields.

In the Property inspector, in the Char width box, type **30**

When a user enters data in this field, no more than 30 characters will be displayed.

Press (↵ ENTER)

To increase the width of the text field.

ACA objectives 4.11a, 4.11b

6	Give the Last name, Address, City, and Email fields the same width value	In the Char width box for each input field, enter 30.
7	Set the width of the State and Zip Code fields to **10**	
8	Scroll down to view the other table	Under the Preferences heading.
9	Drag to the cell below Comments or questions	(The Textarea button.) To insert a textarea field.
	In the ID box, type **Comments**	
	Click **OK**	
10	Click the textarea field	To select it.
11	Set the width of the textarea field to **50**	
	Edit the Num lines box to read **8**	To increase the textarea field's height (the number of lines).
12	Save the page	

List boxes and menus

Explanation
List boxes and menus allow a user to select one or more items from a list. As shown in Exhibit 3-3, a list box displays a fixed number of rows. If the number of items in the list box is greater than the specified height, a scrollbar appears to allow the user to access all of the items in the list.

A menu displays only one item at a time until a user clicks it, thereby displaying the entire menu. Menus enable you to save space on a page. If you have many items in a list or menu, you probably won't want all of them to appear by default. In a menu, a scrollbar appears only if the menu is so long that it occupies the entire screen. The menu form element is also commonly called a *pop-up menu* or *drop-down menu*.

Exhibit 3-3: A list box (left) and a menu (right)

To insert a list box or a menu:

1   Place the insertion point on the page and click the List/Menu button in the Forms category of the Insert panel; or drag the button to the desired location on the page.

2   In the Property inspector, enter a name for the element, if you did not already specify an ID.

3   Select Menu or List to define the type of form element.

4   If you selected List:

  • In the Height box, enter the number of lines to be displayed on the page.

  • Next to Selections, select "Allow multiple" if you want the user to be able to select more than one item in the list.

5   Click List Values and use the List Values dialog box to populate the list or menu. The item label appears on the page; the value is passed to the server. Use the arrow buttons to rearrange the items, if necessary. Then click OK.

6   If you want the list or menu to have a default selection (for example, a default value might be "Select an item from the list"), select it in the "Initially selected" box in the Property inspector.

Do it!

A-3: Creating a list box and a menu

Here's how	Here's why
1 Scroll up	To view the first table in the form.
Drag [icon] to the cell next to the Country prompt	(Scroll down in the Insert panel to locate the List/Menu button.) You'll create a menu.
In the ID box, type **Country**	
Click **OK**	
2 Select the Country input field	If necessary.
In the Property inspector, verify that **Menu** is selected	
3 Click **List Values**	To open the List Values dialog box.
Type **Canada**	This text will appear as an option in the menu.
Press (TAB)	
Type **CAN**	This value will not be seen by the user—it's the value that will be passed to the server if this item is selected. (CAN is the official ISO abbreviation for Canada.)
4 Press (TAB)	
Add the item label **Mexico** with the value **MEX**	
5 Add the item label **United States** with the value **USA**	
Click **OK**	
6 Save the page and preview it in Internet Explorer	
Observe the Country menu	Canada is displayed by default because it's the first item. However, you can set a default selection regardless of its position in the list.
Click the menu	To see the three options in it.
Close the browser	

ACA objectives 4.11a, 4.11b

After students click OK, the insertion point might go to the top of the page. Tell them to select the List/Menu field.

TIPS *Remind students that they can press F12 to open a page in a browser.*

List Values dialog:
Item Label / Value
Canada / CAN
Mexico / MEX
United States / USA

7	In the Initially selected box, select **United States**	In the Property inspector.
	Save the page and preview it in Internet Explorer	The default selection is now United States.
	Close the browser	
8	Under the Preferences heading, place the insertion point as shown	
9	In the Insert panel, click	To insert a List/Menu box.
	In the ID box, type **Publications**, and click **OK**	
10	Select the List/Menu box	If necessary.
	In the Property inspector, select **List**	To create a list rather than a menu. A list displays all of the list items in a box, which might have a scrollbar, depending on the number of items and the height of the list box.
	In the Height box, enter **3**	Three options will be visible in the box.
	Next to Selections, check **Allow multiple**	To allow more than one selection.
11	Click **List Values**	To open the List Values dialog box.
	Populate the list as shown	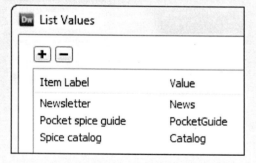
	Click **OK**	
12	Observe the list box on the page	The width of the list box expands to accommodate the widest item label.
13	Save the page and preview it in Internet Explorer	(Press F12.) The first item in the list appears as the default selection.
	Close the browser	

Students want the user to be able to select more than one item in this list.

Check boxes and radio buttons

Explanation   Check boxes allow a user to select one or more items. Radio buttons are usually grouped to allow only one selection, so that clicking one radio button clears the others in its group. For example, you'd want to use radio buttons to obtain gender information because the two options are mutually exclusive.

Creating check boxes

To insert a check box:

1   Place the insertion point on the page and click the Checkbox button in the Insert panel; or drag the button to the desired location on the page.
2   In the Property inspector, enter a unique name for the check box, if you did not already specify an ID.
3   In the Checked value box, enter the value to be passed to the Web server when the box is checked.
4   Select Checked or Unchecked to set the check box's initial state.

Entering values for check boxes

When entering values for your check box items, think of how the data are to be submitted to the server. In many cases, it makes sense to give check boxes a Yes value. For example, if a series of check boxes is meant to obtain user preferences, you might write options such as "send me coupons" (with a field name of Coupons) and "send me information on promotions" (with a field name of Promos). If you give both of these check boxes a Yes value, the information sent to the server will be `coupons="yes"` and/or `promos="yes"`. If a check box is left unchecked, no data is submitted, so it isn't necessary to create No values.

Creating radio buttons

To insert a radio button:

1   Place the insertion point on the page and click the Radio Button icon in the Insert panel; or drag the icon to the desired location on the page.
2   In the Property inspector, enter a name for the radio button, if you did not already specify an ID.
3   In the Checked value box, enter the value to be passed to the Web server when the radio button is selected.
4   Select Checked or Unchecked to set the radio button's initial state.

Radio buttons that have the same name are members of the same group. That is, when one is checked, all the others are cleared, making it impossible for users to select more than one radio button at a time.

Form usability and accessibility

ACA objective 2.4a

The `<label>` element of HTML can make your form inputs easier to select. It can enhance a form's accessibility for visually impaired users, who commonly use screen readers to access Web content.

Matching for and id attributes

If you use the `<label>` element to define your text prompts, users can click the prompt to activate its associated input field. This is a standard user interface convention found in most software applications, and it provides a larger clicking area, making the form easier to use. It also allows users with non-visual browsers, like screen readers, to directly associate a text prompt with its proper input field.

To make this feature work, you use the `for` attribute of the `<label>` tag, matching its value with that of its input ID. For example:

```
<label for="firstName">First Name:</label>
```

This label must then match the ID of its corresponding input field; for example:

```
<input id="firstName" type="text" name="firstName">
```

You can enter this code directly in Code view, or you can use the Input Tag Accessibility Attributes dialog box. When you drag a form input onto a page, this dialog box opens by default (you can disable it). Enter the input's ID in the ID box, and then enter your text prompt in the Label box. Finally, select "Attach label tag using 'for' attribute" to bind the label to the form input.

Do it!   **A-4:   Adding check boxes and radio buttons**

Here's how	Here's why

ACA objectives 4.11a, 4.11b

The page does not contain label elements for the check boxes or radio buttons. Students will create labels in the Input Tag Accessibility Attributes dialog box.

1 Drag  into the second row under Preferences, as shown

(The Checkbox button.) To insert a check box.

In the ID box, type **Specials**

In the Label box, type **Price specials**

2 Select **Attach label tag using 'for' attribute**

Selecting this option creates a text label for the check box and associates it with the ID.

Click **OK**

The label text appears next to the check box.

ACA objective 2.4a

3 Switch to Code view

To observe the label code. The `for` attribute matches the check box's ID. This matching allows non-visual browsers like screen readers to make a direct association between a label and its form input.

⚠ *Tell students that it's important that they place the insertion point here so they don't insert another check box into the same label element. Sometimes you need to use Code view or Split view to place the insertion point properly when you're adding elements.*

Click to the right of the closing `</label>` tag, as shown

`Price specials</label></td>`

You'll insert another check box here.

Click (SPACEBAR)

To add a space to the right of the `</label>` tag.

4 Switch to Design view

5	Click ☑	To insert another check box.
	Set the ID to **Events**	
	Make the label read **Events near me**	
	Verify that **Attach label tag using 'for' attribute** is selected	
	Click **OK**	
6	Select the first check box	For Price specials.
	In the Checked value box, enter **yes**	(In the Property inspector.) If a user checks this box, the name/value pair Specials="yes" will be sent to the database.
7	Set the other check box value to **yes**	
8	Scroll to the top of the page	
9	Drag ◉ to the cell next to the Gender prompt	Scroll down the Insert panel, if necessary.
	In the ID box, type **Male**	
	In the Label box, type **Male**	
	Verify that **Attach label tag using 'for' attribute** is selected	
	Click **OK**	
10	Select the radio button	
	Observe the Property inspector	By default, the radio button is given the default name "radio."
11	Name the radio button **Gender**	 (In the Property inspector.) You'll do the same for the other radio button.
12	Switch to Code view	
	Click to the right of the closing `</label>` tag, as shown	`<label for="Male">Male</label></td>` You'll insert another radio button here.
	Click (SPACEBAR)	To add a space to the right of the tag.

Point out that there's no noticeable result when you enter a value for a form element.

Point out that radio buttons should be used for any mutually exclusive options, such as Yes or No.

⚠ *If students don't switch to Design view before inserting the next radio button, the Tag Editor dialog box will open, and it does not contain the same options.*

13 Switch to Design view

14 To the right of the Male label, insert another radio button

Set the ID and label to **Female** and click **OK**

15 Name the radio button **Gender**   (Select it first.) To give it the same name as the other radio button, making them mutually exclusive.

16 Save the page and preview it in Internet Explorer

Point out that students can click the radio buttons directly, too.

ACA objective 2.4a

17 Click the text **Male**   The radio button is selected when you click its label. This usability enhancement is made possible by the label element's `for` attribute matching the input's ID.

Click the text **Female**   The Male option is deselected.

18 Scroll down the page

If clicking a label doesn't select its input, it's because the second input was inserted into the other input field's label element, which is invalid.

Click the text **Price Specials**   To select the check box. Again, the label text is able to activate the input because the value of the `for` attribute matches the input's ID.

Click the text **Events near me**   To select the check box.

Click it again   To deselect it.

19 Click **Newsletter**   To select the option in the list.

Press ⌷CTRL⌷

Click **Spice catalog**   To select it and Newsletter simultaneously.

20 Type some text in the textarea field   To test the functionality of the textarea field. The text automatically wraps to the next line when it reaches the end.

To complete the form, students need to create a Submit button.

21 Close the browser   Next, you'll add Submit and Reset buttons to the form.

Submit and Reset buttons

Explanation   Without a Submit button, a Web form isn't truly functional. A Submit button allows users to submit their information for processing and storage in a database. A Reset button allows users to clear all form fields if they want to start over.

To add a Submit or Reset button:

1   Place the insertion point on the page and click the Button icon in the Insert panel; or drag the icon to the desired location on the page.
2   In the Property inspector, next to Action, select Submit form or Reset form.
3   Enter a unique name for the button.

Setting up a form to submit data

ACA objective 4.11c   For a form to be operable, it must send the user data to an action page or script for processing. You specify this information by using the Method and Action attributes.

First, select the form container. Then, from the Method pop-up menu in the Property inspector, choose either POST or GET. The GET method appends the user's entered values to the URL, using name/value pairs. The POST method embeds the user's entered values in the HTTP request.

In addition to establishing the method used to submit the form data, you must point the form to the action page or script that processes the data. In the Action box in the Property inspector, enter the path and file name of the action page or script. When the user submits the form data, this page or script processes the data, returning a result or confirmation and typically storing the information in a database. It's important that you ensure that your pages run on a secure server so that user data is not compromised.

Do it!

A-5: Inserting Submit and Reset buttons

Here's how	Here's why

Tell students that without a Submit button, users can't send their data.

1 Scroll to the bottom of the page

Click below the textarea field — Make sure you click inside the form container, indicated by the dotted red line.

2 Scroll down the Insert panel to locate the Button icon — You'll insert a button that submits the form.

3 Click ▢

In the ID box, type **Submit**, and click **OK** — Buttons don't require labels because the buttons themselves display the text prompts.

Students might need to click it twice to activate its properties in the Property inspector.

4 Click the **Submit** button — (If necessary.) To select it.

In the Property inspector, in the Value box, enter **Send** — The text label changes. ("Submit" is the default label for a button.)

Verify that **Submit form** is selected — Next to Action.

Tell students that a Submit button is a required form component, but a Reset button is optional. Also, tell them that they are not specifying method and action attributes here because form processing is beyond the scope of the course.

5 Drag ▢ to the right of the Send button — You'll also create an optional Reset button.

In the ID box, type **Reset**, and click **OK**

Students might need to click the button twice to activate its properties in the Property inspector.

6 Select the **Reset** button

In the Value box, enter **Clear form**

Next to Action, select **Reset form**

Action ○ Submit form
⦿ Reset form

7 Save the page and preview it in Internet Explorer

Fill out some of the form fields

Click **Clear form** — All of the form entries are cleared.

8 Close the browser — To return to Dreamweaver.

9 Close info.html

Customizing the tab order

Explanation

ACA objective 2.4a

Users can navigate through form fields by pressing the Tab key. The *tab order* is the order in which the insertion point jumps from input field to input field as the user presses the Tab key. By default, input fields tab in the order in which they appear in the code. Sometimes this default tab order isn't the best or intended sequence. Depending on the way you design a form, you might need to change the default tab order. Doing so can optimize the usability of your forms and ensure that users with screen readers and other accessibility devices can successfully use the form.

Do it!

A-6:   Observing the default tab order for a form

The files for this activity are in Student Data folder **Unit 3\Topic A**.

Here's how	Here's why
1 Open order.html	This page contains a form for ordering products online.
2 Preview the page in Internet Explorer	
3 In the Billing section, select a card type from the Card Type list	You'll test the default tab order in this section of the form.
Press (TAB)	The insertion point moves to the Full Name field.
Press (TAB)	The insertion point moves to the Card No field.
4 Does the default tab order of this form make sense?	*Not really. Most people would want to complete one section before starting another.*
5 Close the browser	

Setting the tab order of input fields

Explanation

ACA objective 2.4a

If your form's default tab order does not result in a logical flow from one input field to the next, you can customize the order to improve the form's usability and accessibility.

To define the tab order of a form input field:
1 Right-click the field and choose Edit Tag to open the Tag Editor dialog box.
2 Select Style Sheet/Accessibility to display the options in that category.
3 In the Tab Index box, enter the number that represents the position you want the field to occupy in the sequence.
4 Click OK.

To make an input field the first field in a tabbing sequence, enter the number 1 in the Tab Index box. Proceed through 2, 3, and so on for each field, as needed. If you set a tab order, be sure to set Tab Index values for *all* form fields. Otherwise, the tab order might not follow the intended sequence.

Do it!

A-7: Setting the tab order for form fields

Here's how	Here's why
1 Right-click the Card Type field	You'll change the tab order so that all of the fields in the Billing section are selected before the fields in the Shipping section.
Choose **Edit Tag <select>...**	To open the Tag Editor dialog box.
2 Select **Style Sheet/Accessibility**	
In the Tab index box, enter **1** and click **OK**	You'll assign a tab index value to the remaining input fields.
3 Set the Tab index for the Card Number field to **2**	Right-click the field, choose Edit Tag <input>, select Style Sheet/Accessibility, enter 2 in the Tab index box, and click OK.
4 Set the tab order for the other two fields under Billing to **3** and **4**	
5 Set the tab order for the fields in the Shipping section, starting at **5**	Begin by setting the Full Name field's tab index to 5, and then number the remaining fields sequentially.
6 Set the tab order for the two buttons	
7 Save the page and preview it in Internet Explorer	
8 In the Billing section, select a card type from the Card Type list	
9 Press (TAB)	The insertion point moves to the Card Number field, which is a more logical sequence for this form.
Press (TAB)	The insertion point moves to the Exp Date field.
Tab through the rest of the fields	To test the results.
10 Close the browser	
11 Close order.html	

ACA objective 2.4a

If students specified the tab order for the entire form, have them tab through all of the fields.

The Spry framework

Explanation

Dreamweaver's Spry framework enables you to incorporate interactive functionality in your pages without having to get your hands on any scripting code. The *Spry framework* is a library of HTML, CSS, and JavaScript code that provides a variety of interactive components, such as dynamic navigation menus, data sets, and form input fields that validate data.

Spry widgets

Spry widgets are elements that you can insert in a page the same way you insert other elements, like images and tables. Using Spry widgets, you can quickly create interactive components without having scripting experience. Spry widgets are composed of HTML, CSS, and JavaScript. When you use a Spry widget for the first time, Dreamweaver creates a folder in your site that stores the Spry assets.

When you add a Spry widget to a page, links to the associated Spry assets (JavaScript and CSS files) are created automatically, and the file names appear at the top of the Document window. The files are named after the widget. You can edit the file names, as well as the HTML, CSS, and JavaScript code, as needed to customize a widget. Click a file name at the top of the Document window to open the file.

The Validation Text Field widget

There are many Spry widgets that you can use in place of standard form input elements. With the Spry Validation Text Field widget, you can create text fields that validate user entries. For example, you can set the widget to ensure that users enter a date in a valid date format that matches the format used in your database. If a user enters a date in an invalid format, the widget produces an error message on the page. The error messages that Spry widgets display are built with HTML and CSS, so you can edit and customize them just like any other content on your pages.

Setting the validation trigger

After you insert a Spry widget, you can set its properties in the Property inspector. One of these properties is the *trigger event* for the validation script. For example, you can set the validation to occur when the user types in a field, clicks away from a field, or clicks the Submit button.

Live View

ACA objective 3.1b

In Dreamweaver CS5, you can view and test pages that contain dynamic and interactive content without having to first set up a testing server. You can use Live View to test your Spry widgets, rollovers, and applications without having to deal with Web server connectivity and maintenance. Live View also provides a quick alternative to previewing a page in a browser. Live View uses the same rendering engine used by several current browsers, so you can be sure that you're seeing an accurate representation of how your page will look and function when it's live on the Web.

While in Live View, you can also activate Live Code view, which splits the Document window into two panes so you can interact with page elements and see the results in the code. You can also make changes in Live Code view and see the results in the Live View pane.

Do it! **A-8: Creating and modifying a Spry widget**

The files for this activity are in Student Data folder **Unit 3\Topic A**.

Here's how	Here's why
1 Open signup.html	(From the Files panel.) The page contains a nearly completed form. You'll add two validation fields.
2 Click in the cell next to the Zip Code prompt	State: ▢ Zip Code: | To place the insertion point.
3 In the Insert panel, click **Forms** and select **Spry**	To display the Spry tools in the Insert panel.
4 Click **Spry Validation Text Field**	The Input Tag Accessibility Attributes dialog box opens.
In the ID box, type **Zip**	
Select **No label tag**	There's already a text prompt for this input field.
Click **OK**	State: ▢ Spry TextField: sprytextfield1 Zip Code: ▢ A Spry TextField widget appears on the page.
5 Set the width of the field to **10**	Select the text field and enter 10 in the Char width box in the Property inspector.
6 Click the **Spry TextField** tab	State: ▢ Spry TextField: sprytextfield1 Zip Code: ▢ To select the Spry widget and display its properties in the Property inspector.
Name the widget **SpryZip** as shown	PROPERTIES Spry TextField SpryZip
7 From the Type list, select **Zip Code**	The Format list automatically selects US-5. This text field will ensure that the user enters a standard five-digit ZIP code.
Observe the widget on the page	A box saying "Invalid format" appears to the right of the input field. This is the error message that will appear if the user enters invalid data.

	8 In the Property inspector, next to Validate on, check **Blur**	Validate on ☑ Blur
		To set the validation to trigger when the user clicks away from the Zip Code input field.
	9 Verify that **Required** is selected	This ensures that the text field is not left blank when the form is submitted.
Tell students to click OK if a dialog box opens.	10 Save the page	If a Copy Dependent Files dialog box appears, click OK.
	Observe the Related Files toolbar	The document is now linked to two files: SpryValidationTextField.js, a JavaScript file that creates the validation functionality; and a new style sheet (.css file) that controls the error message formatting.
	11 Observe the Files panel	The site now contains a folder named SpryAssets, which holds all of the files that enable the Spry functionality.
ACA objective 3.1b	12 Click Live View	(On the Document toolbar.) To display the page in Live View. This feature allows you to test dynamic functionality, including Spry widgets.
	Scroll down to view the Zip Code field	If necessary.
	13 In the Zip Code field, type six or more numbers	
Point out that clicking away from the field is the validation trigger used when Blur is selected.	Click away from the input field	123456 Invalid format.
		The input field is highlighted and the error message appears next to it. Using Spry validation fields can help ensure that the data you receive from users is accurate and complete.
	14 Click Live View again	To turn off Live View.
	15 Drag to select the error message text	Spry TextField: SpryZip Invalid format
	Type **Enter a valid 5-digit zip code**	Spry TextField: SpryZip Enter a valid 5-digit zip code.
		To customize the error message.

16 Next to the Email prompt, insert a
    Spry Validation Text Field

    Set the ID to **Email**

    Verify that no label will be
    applied, and click **OK**

17 Click the **Spry TextField** tab   (If necessary.) To select the Spry widget.

    Name it **ValidateEmail**

    From the Type list, select
    Email Address

    Next to Validate on, select **Blur**

    Verify that **Required** is selected   To ensure that the text field is not left blank
                                              when the form is submitted.

18 Edit the error message to read
    **Enter a valid email
    address.**

19 Save the page and activate
    Live View

    Scroll to the bottom of the page

    Submit the form   Click the Send button.

    Scroll up to view the error   The messages indicate that these two fields are
    messages   required. This conditional text is automatically
                                              applied when the Required option is selected.

20 Test the Zip Code field   (Type six or more numbers and click away from
                                              the field.) The new error message appears.

Point out that these are   21 In the Email field, enter your   The @ symbol is required for an e-mail address
just a couple examples of   e-mail address but omit the @   to be valid.
the types of data
validation available.   Click away from the Email field   The error message appears.

22 Enter a valid e-mail address and   The error message disappears.
    click away from the field

23 Save and close the file

Unit summary: Forms

Topic A
In this topic, you learned how to create a **form** and add a variety of input fields and controls. You learned how to set **input field properties**, such as height and width, apply labels, and customize the tab order of form input fields to improve **usability** and **accessibility**. Finally, you learned how to use **Spry widgets** to create form input fields that validate user entries to ensure the integrity of data, and you learned how to use **Live View** to see the results of your Spry widgets, rollovers, and dynamic applications.

Independent practice activity

In this activity, you'll add standard input fields and Spry input fields to a form. Then you'll modify the input properties, customize the tab order, and test the form in Live View.

The files for this activity are in Student Data folder **Unit 3\Unit summary**.

1 Create a site named **Forms practice**. Set the Outlander folder as the local root folder. (The Outlander folder is in the current Unit summary folder.)

2 Open login.html. This page contains a form with labeled text prompts. You'll add a variety of input fields to it.

3 Add text input fields for the First name and Last name rows. Give each field a unique and relevant name.

4 Add standard radio buttons to the left of the Male and Female prompts. Give the radio buttons the same name so that selecting one button clears the other.

5 Next to the Email prompt, insert a Spry Validation Text Field. Set the widget to determine whether the entry is a valid e-mail address, and have the validation execute when the user clicks away from the input field.

6 Change the error message to read "Enter a valid e-mail address."

7 Insert a Spry Validation Text Field for the Login name and Password. Verify that both are set as required fields.

8 Insert a drop-down menu in the cell below the question "Where did you first hear of Outlander Spices?" (*Hint:* Drag the List/Menu button from the Forms category of the Insert panel. Then select Menu in the Property inspector.)

9 Add the following items to the menu: **Grocery store**, **Gourmet shop**, **The Web**, **A friend**. Assign a unique value to each selection. (*Hint:* In the Property inspector, click List Values.)

10 Insert check boxes before the choices **Online** and **In grocery stores**, and give each one a unique name and checked value.

11 Insert a textarea field in the row below "Comments or questions." Set the field's width to **55**.

12 Define a logical tab order for every input field and the Submit button.

13 Save the page and test the form in Live View.

14 Close the page.

Review questions

1 True or false? If you define the tab order for one or more input fields, you should define the tab order for *all* input fields in the form.

   True. Otherwise, the tab order might not follow a logical or desirable sequence.

2 What determines the default tab order of a set of form input fields?

   A The default Tab Index values that Dreamweaver automatically applies to each input field

   B The order in which the input fields appear in a browser

   C The order in which the input fields appear in the code

   D Alphabetical order

3 To start a form, you need to:

   A Add input fields.

   B Insert a form container by dragging the Form button to the page or by clicking the Form button while the insertion point is positioned on the page.

   C Clear all other HTML first.

   D Switch to Code view or Split view.

4 Every form input field you create must be given a name so that:

   A You can keep track of each form field.

   B Users can more easily navigate the form.

   C The tab order follows a logical sequence.

   D The information a user enters is submitted to the server as a name/value pair.

5 True or false? All form input fields must be placed inside the `<form>` container.

   True

6 The main difference between check boxes and radio buttons is that:

   A Check boxes are square and radio buttons are round.

   B Radio buttons offer mutually exclusive options, and check boxes don't.

   C Check boxes aren't usually checked by default.

   D Radio buttons aren't usually selected by default.

7 True or false? Without a Submit button, a Web form isn't truly functional.

   True

8 To create accessible form input fields that enable users to click text prompts to activate the corresponding inputs, you need to:

   A Apply IDs to the input fields.

   B Use labels to define the text prompts, and match the value of the `<label>` tag's `for` attribute with the ID of its corresponding input.

   C Use labels to define text prompts, and match the value of the `<label>` tag's `id` attribute with the ID of its corresponding input.

   D Apply IDs to the input labels.

9 True or false? The error messages that Dreamweaver creates when you add Spry validation fields are fully customizable.

True. They are made with HTML and CSS, so you can edit them just like any other page or style sheet content.

10 What is the Spry framework?

A An add-on application that enables you to build dynamic functionality

B Code embedded directly in the page that controls a variety of dynamic and interactive functionality

C A library of HTML, CSS, and JavaScript code that provides a variety of interactive components, such as dynamic navigation menus, data sets, and form input fields that validate data

D An XML library

Unit 4

Rollovers, behaviors, and AP Divs

Unit time: 75 minutes

Complete this unit, and you'll know how to:

A Create rollover images and apply behaviors to page elements.

B Insert AP Divs; adjust the size, position, and visibility of an AP Div; and control layer visibility dynamically.

Topic A: Applying rollovers and behaviors

This topic covers the following Adobe ACA exam objectives for Dreamweaver CS5.

#	Objective
3.1b	Demonstrate knowledge of the differences between Design view, Code view, Split view, and Live view.
4.4b	Demonstrate knowledge of how to add alternative text to images by using the Image Tag Accessibility Attributes dialog box or the Property inspector.
4.7a	Demonstrate knowledge of how to insert navigation bars, rollover images, and buttons created in Fireworks.

Rollovers

Explanation

Rollovers provide visual feedback for a user's actions and can improve usability while enhancing the appeal of your interface design. A *rollover* swaps a primary image (the initial image that's displayed when the page loads) with a secondary image. A rollover is triggered by an *event*, which is most commonly the user pointing to the primary image. Other events include clicking an element or clicking away from an element.

The primary and secondary images of a rollover should be the same height and width. File sizes can be slightly different, but the dimensions of the two images should be identical to prevent distortion and to ensure a smooth transition between the images.

Creating a rollover

To create a rollover:

1 Place the insertion point on the page.

2 In the Insert panel, select the Common category.

3 Click the black triangle next to the Images button and select Rollover Image to open the Insert Rollover Image dialog box, shown in Exhibit 4-1.

4 In the Image name box, enter a name for the rollover.

5 Next to the Original image box, click Browse and select the primary image.

6 Next to the Rollover image box, click Browse and select the secondary image.

7 Verify that "Preload rollover image" is selected.

ACA objective 4.4b

8 In the Alternate text box, type alternate text, which will appear if the browser can't display the image(s). Alternate text can also be read by screen readers and other alternative browsing devices.

9 Click OK.

Exhibit 4-1: The Insert Rollover Image dialog box

JavaScript

JavaScript is a scripting language you can use to add interactivity and functionality to your Web pages. JavaScript is client-side code, rather than server-side. This means that it executes directly in the browser and does not require interaction with a server.

Scripts are often written directly in a Web page's `<head>` section. If you want a script to apply to multiple pages, you can create an external JavaScript file and link the pages to it, similar to the way pages are linked to an external style sheet.

Rollovers are built with JavaScript. Dreamweaver writes the required JavaScript code automatically.

Adding content from Fireworks

ACA objective 4.7a

You can easily insert content that was created in Adobe Fireworks, such as navigation bars, pop-up menus, and rollovers. To insert content exported from Fireworks, place the insertion point on the page. Then either choose Insert, Image Objects, Fireworks HTML, or click the Image button in the Common category of the Insert panel and choose Insert Fireworks HTML. Then click Browse, navigate to the Fireworks-exported file, select it, and click OK. Dreamweaver imports all components of the Fireworks object, which can include HTML code, images, and JavaScript.

Do it!

A-1: Applying rollover images

The files for this activity are in Student Data folder **Unit 4\Topic A**.

Here's how	Here's why
1 Choose **Site, New Site...**	To open the Site Setup dialog box.
2 In the Site Name box, type **Rollovers**	To name the site.
3 Browse to the current topic folder	Student Data folder Unit 4\Topic A.
Open the Outlander folder, click **Select**, and then click **Save**	To set the root folder for this site and create the site.
4 Open gallery.html	You'll create a navigation bar with rollover images.
5 Triple-click the text shown	Insert left nav bar here
	To select it.
Press DELETE	
6 In the Insert panel, select the **Common** category	If necessary.
7 Click **Images**	To display the image options.
Select **Rollover Image**	To open the Insert Rollover Image dialog box. You'll create rollover images in a navigation bar format.
In the Image name box, type **cinnamon**	
8 Next to the Original image box, click **Browse...**	To open the Original Image dialog box.
Open the images folder	
Select **cinnamontext.gif** and click **OK**	Scroll down.

Students will build an image gallery by using the Navigation Bar component.

9 Next to the Rollover image box, click **Browse...**

Select **cinnamontextglow.gif** and click **OK**

Image name:	cinnamon
Original image:	images/cinnamontext.gif
Rollover image:	images/cinnamontextglow.gif
	☑ Preload rollover image

ACA objective 4.4b

In the Alternate text box, type **cinnamon**

To provide alternate text for text-only browsers, screen readers, and other alternative browsing devices.

Click **OK**

The cinnamontext.gif image appears on the page.

10 Click to the right of the cinnamon text image, as shown

Cinnamon [

Press (↵ ENTER)

You'll insert another rollover image on the next line.

Point out that this method is an alternative to using the button in the Insert panel.

11 Choose **Insert**, **Image Objects**, **Rollover Image**

To open the Insert Rollover Image dialog box again.

Type **cloves**

To name the new item.

Set the Original image to **clovestext.gif**

In the images folder, in the Outlander folder.

Set the Rollover image to **clovestextglow.gif**

In the Alternate text box, type **cloves** and click **OK**

12 Start a new line under the cloves image

Click to the right of the Cloves text image and press Enter.

Open the Insert Rollover Image dialog box

Use either the button in the Insert panel or the Insert menu.

13 Type **coriander**

Set the Original image to **coriandertext.gif**

Set the Rollover image to **coriandertextglow.gif**

Point out that if students were building an actual navigation bar, they would need to enter the URL of the destination page or resource for each rollover in the "When clicked, Go to URL" box.	14 Verify that **Preload rollover image** is selected	This setting makes the rollover images load when the page opens, rather than when the mouse pointer first moves over the rollover image. If this option isn't selected, the user might notice a delay while the image loads.
	Enter alternate text and click **OK**	
	15 Save the page	
ACA objective 3.1b	16 Click Live View	In Live View, you can test the rollovers without having to open a browser.
	Point to the spice names	When you move the pointer over an image, it changes to the Rollover image, creating the illusion that the text itself is changing. When the pointer moves off the spice name, the image reverts to the original.
	Click Live View	To deactivate Live View.
ACA objective 4.7a *Facilitate a brief discussion. Fireworks and Dreamweaver are often used together.*	17 How can you insert rollovers created in Adobe Fireworks?	*Place the insertion point on the page where you want to insert the content. Then either choose Insert, Image Objects, Fireworks HTML, or click the Image button in the Common category of the Insert panel and choose Insert Fireworks HTML.*

Behaviors

Explanation

Behaviors allow a user to interact with a page in a variety of ways. Behaviors are a combination of an *event*, which is typically triggered by the user, and an *action*, which occurs in response to the event. Dreamweaver provides several built-in behaviors that you can access in the Tag inspector.

To attach a behavior to an element:

1 Select an element on the page to serve as the event trigger.
2 Choose Window, Behaviors to activate the Tag inspector in Behaviors mode.
3 Click the Add behavior button (the plus sign) and select a behavior from the list. A dialog box specific to that behavior opens.
4 Use the fields and controls in the dialog box to define the behavior.
5 Click OK.

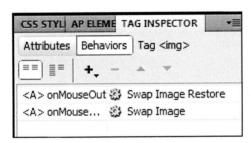

Exhibit 4-2: The Tag inspector in Behaviors mode, showing two behaviors

The Swap Image behavior

The *Swap Image* behavior uses a trigger event to cause changes in one or more other images on the page. The trigger object itself doesn't change unless it has been assigned its own rollover.

To apply a Swap Image behavior:

1 On the page, select an image to serve as the trigger object.
2 Choose Window, Behaviors to open the Tag inspector in Behaviors mode.
3 Click the Add behavior button and choose Swap Image to open the Swap Image dialog box.
4 From the Images list, select the image to be replaced.
5 Next to the "Set source to" box, click Browse and select a secondary image.
6 Verify that "Preload images" is checked.
7 Verify that "Restore images onMouseOut" is selected.
8 Click OK.

Dreamweaver's built-in behaviors are client-side scripts—they execute in the browser without any server interaction. However, Dreamweaver also provides several server behaviors, which you can access by choosing Window, Server Behaviors. The Server Behaviors panel contains several built-in behaviors that you can use to display content from external data sources, like databases and server objects, and to create a variety of powerful applications written in ColdFusion, ASP, or PHP. To access server behaviors, you first need to establish a connection to a server.

A-2:   Applying the Swap Image behavior

Live View is not active.

TIPS
Students can also press Shift+F4.

Here's how	Here's why
1 On the page, click the Cinnamon text image	To select it. You'll add a Swap Image action to the spice names so that their corresponding images appear in place of the default spice image on the page.
2 Choose **Window**, **Behaviors**	To open the Tag inspector in Behaviors mode. Two actions are already associated with the image. These were added when you created the rollover images.
Click [**+**]	The Add behavior button.
Choose **Swap Image**	To open the Swap Image dialog box.
3 From the Images list, select **image "spices"**	To select the image you want to replace (the image of the spices in the middle of the page).
Click **Browse...**	To open the Select Image Source dialog box.
Select **cinnamon_lg.jpg**	To replace the spices image with a large image of cinnamon.
Click **OK**	An asterisk appears next to *image "spices"* in the Images list, indicating that an action has been applied.
4 Verify that **Preload images** is checked	
Click **OK**	To close the dialog box and add the behavior.
5 Click the Cloves text image	To select it.
6 Apply the **Swap Image** behavior to the image	In the Tag inspector, click the Add behavior button and select Swap Image.
Swap the spices image with cloves_lg.jpg	In the Images list, select *image "spices"*. Click Browse and select cloves_lg.jpg.
Click **OK**	
7 Add the **Swap Image** behavior to the Coriander text image	
Swap the spices image with coriander_lg.jpg	

8 Save the page	
Activate Live View	You'll verify the results.
Point to the spice names	The corresponding image appears when you point to each spice name.
9 Deactivate Live View	Click the Live View button again.
Close gallery.html	

Topic B: Creating and modifying AP Divs

This topic covers the following Adobe ACA exam objectives for Dreamweaver CS5.

#	Objective
4.4b	Demonstrate knowledge of how to add alternative text to images by using the Image Tag Accessibility Attributes dialog box or the Property inspector.
5.2b	Demonstrate knowledge of the advantages of using Div tags instead of tables for page layout.
5.2c	Demonstrate knowledge of the distinctions among absolute, relative, fixed, and static positioning.
5.2e	Demonstrate knowledge of how to modify Div tag attributes.
5.2f	Demonstrate knowledge of how to display overlapping content on a Web page using Div tags.

AP elements and positioning

Explanation

Positioning is a category of CSS specific to page layout and the precise arrangement of page elements. Positioned elements are usually Div tags, but any displayed content can be an AP (absolutely positioned) element.

The AP Elements panel

Any element that's absolutely positioned is considered an *AP element* and will appear in the AP Elements panel. With the AP Elements panel, you can select AP elements, control their stacking order, and set visibility properties. To open the AP Elements panel, choose Window, AP Elements. In Design view, you can draw AP Divs directly on a page, and then move and resize them as needed.

CSS positioning

ACA objective 5.2c

CSS positioning is a layout method that provides precise control over the arrangement of page elements. There are four types of positioning:

- **Absolute positioning** — Places an element at exact pixel coordinates based on the top-left corner of the browser window. Absolutely positioned elements remain set in their positions on a page, and those positions don't change as new content is added or arranged. All absolutely positioned elements appear in the AP Elements panel.

- **Fixed positioning** — Is a subcategory of absolute positioning. The only difference is that a fixed-position element doesn't scroll with the document—the positioning coordinates are fixed to the browser window.

- **Relative positioning** — Arranges an element relative to its normal location in the document flow. In other words, a relatively positioned element is positioned relative to the location it would normally occupy if it weren't positioned. Relatively positioned elements do not appear in the AP Elements panel.

- **Static positioning** — Displays an element in its normal location in the document. This option is the same as not specifying any positioning value, so its use is limited to dynamic scripting, where you might need to turn off an element's positioning if certain conditions are met.

Page layout using AP Divs

ACA objective 5.2b

AP Divs—absolutely positioned Div tags—serve as containers for content that you can position on a page with pixel-level precision. Using AP Divs to establish a layout is far more efficient and effective than using HTML tables for layout. Using HTML tables for the purpose of arranging content is less precise, and it requires a lot of HTML code, which has to be repeated—consistently—on each page. This method leads to pages that are built with a lot of unnecessary clutter and are difficult to update and troubleshoot.

When you arrange your content regions with Div tags that are positioned with CSS, each document requires a minimum amount of code; all layout and style rules can be stored in one external style sheet that all site documents can share. Site pages then load quickly and can be efficiently indexed by search engines. In addition, you can overlap AP Divs—which are also called *layers*—and this capability enables you to create designs that can't be achieved with HTML tables.

Overlapping AP elements

ACA objective 5.2f

You can arrange AP elements on a page so that certain areas overlap. This capability can provide a lot of design flexibility and creative opportunities. You use the z-index value to control how an AP element overlaps other AP elements.

An AP element's *z-index* value defines the element's "depth" relative to other AP elements on the page. The z-index depth is also called the *stacking order;* AP elements may overlap, so the z-index value determines which elements appear on top of others. The higher the integer value, the higher that AP element appears in the stacking order, as illustrated in Exhibit 4-3. Z-index values do not need to be sequential. For example, if you want to ensure that an element is at the top of the stacking order, you can give it a z-index value of 100 or some other value that's much higher than that of the other AP elements.

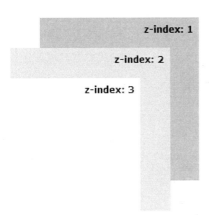

Exhibit 4-3: Three overlapping AP elements with different z-index values

Inserting AP Divs

To insert an AP Div, do any of the following:

- Click to place the insertion point where you want it on the page, and then choose Insert, Layout Objects, AP Div.
- Use the Draw AP Div tool. In the Layout category of the Insert panel, click the Draw AP Div button and then drag on the page to draw the AP Div. You can press and hold the Control key to draw multiple AP Divs.
- Drag the Draw AP Div button itself onto the page. An AP Div container will appear wherever you release the mouse button.

After you've created an AP Div, you can click inside it to place the insertion point and then add whatever content you need.

When you create an AP Div, Dreamweaver inserts a `<div>` tag in the HTML code and assigns a default ID to it. Dreamweaver also embeds CSS rules in the document's `<head>` section to control the position and dimensions of the AP Div. Exhibit 4-4 shows an example of the HTML code that Dreamweaver writes when you create an AP Div. Exhibit 4-5 shows an example of the corresponding CSS code that controls the AP Div's size and position on the page.

```
<div id="apDiv1">
Content of apDiv 1...
</div>

<div id="apDiv2">
Content of apDiv 2...
</div>
```

Exhibit 4-4: An example of the HTML positioning styles for two AP Divs

```
#apDiv1 {
    position:absolute;
    left:129px;
    top:292px;
    width:226px;
    height:109px;
    z-index:2;
}
#apDiv2 {
    position:absolute;
    width:105px;
    height:64px;
    z-index:3;
    left: 404px;
    top: 485px;
}
```

Exhibit 4-5: An example of absolute positioning rules controlling AP Divs

Do it!

B-1:   Inserting AP Divs

The files for this activity are in Student Data folder **Unit 4\Topic B**.

Here's how	Here's why
1 Choose **Site**, **New Site...**	To open the Site Setup dialog box.
2 In the Site Name box, type **AP Divs**	To name the site.
3 Browse to the current topic folder	Student Data folder Unit 4\Topic B.
Open the Outlander folder, click **Select**, and then click **Save**	To set the root folder for this site and create the site.
4 Open heatquiz.html	(From the Files panel.) You'll use AP Divs to create a dynamic feature on this page. You'll begin by adding a large heat graph as a background image.
Verify that Design view is active	
5 In the Insert panel, select the **Layout** category	
In the Insert panel, click	The Draw AP Div button.

Tell students to draw the container in the indicated position on the page, but the exact size doesn't matter.

Drag on the page to create a rectangular container, as shown	To draw an AP Div.

Point to a pepper name (at left) to show it on the graph be order, from least hot to hottest. Have fun!

Cayenne
Habanero
Chipotle
Pepperonicini

6 In the Files panel, expand the images folder

Expand the heatgraph_images folder

7 Drag **heatgraph.jpg** into the AP Div, as shown

When you release the mouse button, the Image Tag Accessibility Attributes dialog box appears.

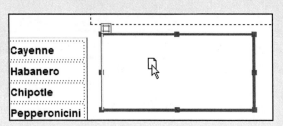

ACA objective 4.4b

In the Alternate text box, enter **Scoville heat graph**

To provide alternate text for visually impaired users who access Web content with screen readers and other accessibility devices.

Click **OK**

When you insert an image that's larger than the AP Div, the container resizes automatically. Therefore, the size of the container isn't important when you draw it. You can also resize it manually.

Point out that the AP Div is overlapping the heat graph image. This is an example of layout techniques you can use with AP Divs.

8 Drag the Draw AP Div button onto the heat graph image

To create an AP Div. Dreamweaver creates a container and gives it a default ID.

9 Drag cayenne.gif into the AP Div

(From the heatgraph_images folder.) The Image Tag Accessibility Attributes dialog box appears.

In the Alternate text box, type **Cayenne**

Click **OK**

Students will continue to build this page in the next activity.

10 Save the page

Next, you'll add more AP Divs, arrange them on the page, and change their settings.

Selecting and modifying AP Divs

Explanation

After you create an AP Div, you can resize it, move it anywhere on a page, rename it, and apply other properties. When an AP Div is selected, you can point to it to view its properties. You can point to its border to view its margin, border, and padding values. You can also use the Property inspector to view its properties.

To modify an AP Div, you must first select it. There are several ways you can select an AP Div:

- Click inside the AP Div and then click its selection handle.
- Click the border of the AP Div.
- Press Ctrl+Shift and click inside the AP Div.
- Click inside the AP Div and press Ctrl+A.
- Click inside the AP Div and then click its tag in the Tag selector.
- In the AP Elements panel, click the AP Div's name.

To select multiple AP Divs, do either of the following:

- Shift+click inside or on the border of two or more AP Divs.
- In the AP Elements panel, Shift+click the names of two or more AP Divs.

Moving an AP Div

To move an AP Div, select it and do any of the following:

- Drag from the selection handle.
- Point to any border until the pointer changes to a four-headed arrow, and then drag.
- Press an arrow key to move the AP Div one pixel at a time.
- Hold down Shift and press an arrow key to move the AP Div one grid increment at a time.

Resizing an AP Div

To resize an AP Div, select it and do any of the following:

- Drag any of the AP Div's resize handles.
- Hold down Ctrl and press the arrow keys to resize the AP Div, one pixel at a time, by moving its right and bottom borders.
- Hold down Shift+Ctrl and press the arrow keys to resize the AP DIV, one grid increment at a time, by moving the right and bottom borders.
- In the Property inspector, enter values in the W and H boxes.

Naming an AP Div

To name an AP Div, do either of the following:

- Select an AP Div. In the CSS-P Element box in the Property inspector, enter a name.
- In the AP Elements panel, double-click an AP Div name and edit it.

B-2: Modifying AP Divs

Here's how	Here's why
1 Click an edge of the heat graph AP Div	To select the AP Div, and not the image in it. The AP Div is highlighted with a blue outline, and the selection handle appears in the top-left corner.
2 In the Property inspector, edit the CSS-P Element box to read **Heatgraph**	To replace the default ID with a meaningful ID.
3 Click anywhere in the cayenne layer	("Layer" is another term for AP Div.) The layer's border is highlighted, but the AP Div itself isn't selected—its content is. To modify the AP Div, you need to select it and not its contents.
Click the selection handle, as shown	To select the AP Div itself and not its contents.
4 Give this AP Div the ID **Cayenne**	In the Property inspector, edit the text in the CSS-P Element box.
5 From the selection handle, drag the layer to the position shown	You can also use the arrow keys to move a layer in small increments.

ACA objective 5.2e

Tell students that AP Divs are also referred to as "layers."

⚠ *Tell students to drag from the selection handle, as shown. If they drag the content out of the layer, have them undo their last action and then drag from the selection handle.*

Also, tell them they can use the arrow keys to move a layer incrementally.

	6 Point to the lower-right resize handle	The pointer changes to a diagonal arrow, indicating that you can change the height and width of the layer simultaneously.
ACA objective 5.2f	Drag upward and to the left, as shown	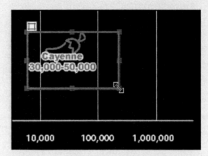
		To resize the layer so that it's only as large as it needs to be to accommodate the image. This can make it easier to work with multiple layers.
Tell students that "names" in the context of AP Divs are synonymous with IDs.	7 On the heat graph, add an AP Div and name it **Habanero**	Drag the Draw AP Div button onto the Heat graph image. Then, in the Property inspector, enter Habanero in the CSS-P Element box.
	Insert habanero.gif into the Habanero layer	The image is in the heatgraph_images folder, in the images folder. Give the image the alternate text "Habanero."
Tell students that it's okay if the layers overlap—they won't be displayed at the same time.	8 Position the Habanero layer as shown	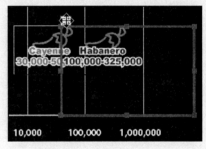
		(Drag from the layer's selection handle.) The pepper in the image should mark the heat rating on the chart. Because these images will ultimately be pop-ups that appear one at a time, it's okay that they overlap.
	Resize the layer	So that it's only as large as it needs to be.
	9 On the heat graph, add an AP Div and name it **Chipotle**	Drag the Draw AP Div button onto the Heat graph image. Then, in the Property inspector, enter Chipotle in the CSS-P Element box.
	Insert chipotle.gif into the Chipotle layer	Be sure to add appropriate alternate text.

10 Position the Chipotle layer as shown

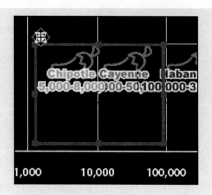

Resize the layer   So that it's only as large as it needs to be.

11 Save the page

Controlling visibility

Explanation

You can show or hide AP elements in Design view so that you can more easily position overlapping AP elements. By showing and hiding AP elements, you can also preview how a page will appear under various conditions.

To hide an AP element, activate the AP Elements panel and click in the Visibility column next to the element you want to hide. A closed-eye icon appears; this indicates that the corresponding layer will not be visible. Click the eye icon again to make the layer visible, as shown in Exhibit 4-6. Layers have no visibility property by default, so if an element does not have an eye icon next to it, it's currently in its default visible state.

To temporarily display and select an AP element in a document, click the element's name in the AP Elements panel.

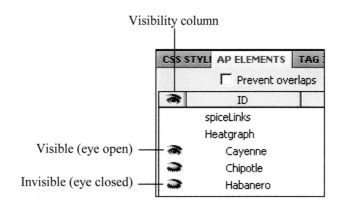

Exhibit 4-6: The AP Elements panel, showing visible and invisible elements

B-3: Setting visibility

Here's how	Here's why
Students will explore the behavior of the visibility property to learn how to work more effectively with AP Divs.	
1 Choose **Window**, **AP Elements**	To open the AP Elements panel. Notice that the spice layers are nested under the Heatgraph layer. This occurs because the layers were originally placed inside the Heatgraph layer. (It's okay if one or more spice layers do not appear under the Heatgraph layer.)
2 Click the Visibility column next to Chipotle, Habanero, and Cayenne, as shown	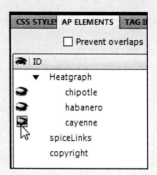
	To hide these three AP elements.
Save the page and then activate Live View	The AP elements are not visible.
Deactivate Live View	(Click the Live View button again.) To return to Design view.
Students might have to scroll down to see the AP Div. 3 In the AP Elements panel, click **Chipotle**	To select it. The AP Div becomes visible on the page, but the visibility icon shows that the element wouldn't be visible in a browser.
In the Document window, click away from the AP Div	To deselect it. The AP Div is invisible again. You can select layers in the AP Elements panel to activate them on the page, but to control their visibility, you must use the Visibility column.
4 Observe the Z column	(In the AP Elements panel.) The Z column displays each layer's z-index value. Z-index values can be duplicated and need not be sequential.
Double-click the Z column next to the Heatgraph layer	To select the value.
Enter **1**	To give the Heatgraph layer a z-index value of 1. This low number will ensure that the other AP elements will be displayed above it.
Give the individual spice layers z-index values greater than 1	The spices will be displayed only one at a time, so it doesn't matter if they have the same value.
5 Save the page	Next, you'll assign behaviors to the AP Divs to control their visibility dynamically.

The Show-Hide Elements behavior

Explanation

With the Show-Hide Elements behavior, you can show, hide, or restore the default visibility of an element. You can use this behavior to dynamically control the visibility of an AP element. For example, you can have an AP Div appear when a user points to an object and disappear when the user points away from the object.

To dynamically control an element's visibility:

1   Select an object on the page to act as a rollover trigger.
2   Choose Window, Behaviors to activate the Tag inspector in Behaviors mode.
3   Click the Add behavior button (the plus sign) and choose Show-Hide Elements to open the Show-Hide Elements dialog box.
4   From the Elements list, select the element you want to show, hide, or restore to default visibility.
5   Click Show, Hide, or Default, and click OK.
6   In the Tag inspector, click the event name to activate the Event list.
7   From the Event list, select the event that you want to trigger the action (if the default event is not the one you want to apply).

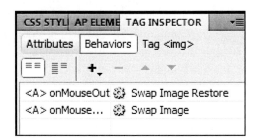

Exhibit 4-7: The Tag inspector in Behaviors mode, showing two behaviors

B-4:   Controlling visibility dynamically

Here's how	Here's why
1 In the spice links layer, select the text **Cayenne**	You'll make this text act as a rollover trigger—the Cayenne layer will appear when a user points to it.
2 Choose **Window, Tag Inspector**	You can also click the Tag Inspector tab, next to the AP Elements tab.
In the Tag inspector, click [**+**]	The Add behavior button.
Choose **Show-Hide Elements**	To open the Show-Hide Elements dialog box.
3 In the Elements list, select **div "Cayenne"**	
Click **Show**	
Click **OK**	The behavior appears in the Tag inspector. Notice that onClick is the default event to trigger the action. You'll change this to a different event.
4 In the Tag inspector, click **onClick**	To activate the Event list. A drop-down arrow appears.
Click the drop-down arrow and scroll down the list	
Select **onMouseOver**	To change the event for this behavior so that the Cayenne layer appears when a user points to the text "Cayenne."
	Next, you'll apply a behavior to make the layer disappear when the mouse isn't over the text.
5 Create a new Show-Hide Elements behavior	Click the Add behavior button and choose Show-Hide Elements.
Select **div "Cayenne"**	
Click **Hide**	
Click **OK**	
Help students with this step, if necessary. 6 From the Event list, select **onMouseOut**	To change the event for this behavior from the default onClick to onMouseOut. This event will hide the layer when the pointer moves away from the text.

7   Activate Live View

    Scroll down to view the whole heat graph image   If necessary.

8   Point to the Cayenne text   The Cayenne layer appears in the graph.

    Point away from the Cayenne text   The Cayenne layer disappears.

    Deactivate Live View

9   Select the text **Habanero**   You'll apply a Show-Hide Elements behavior to the Habanero layer.

    Apply a behavior to show the Habanero layer when a user points to the text   In the Tag inspector, click the Add behavior button and choose Show-Hide Elements. In the dialog box, select *div "Habanero"* and click Show. From the Events list, select onMouseOver.

Remind students to use the onMouseOut event.

    Apply a behavior to hide the Habanero layer when a user points away from the text

Be sure students use the text Chipotle as the trigger object.

10   Apply the same two behaviors to the Chipotle layer

11   Activate Live View

    Test the behaviors and then deactivate Live View   None of the spice images should be displayed by default. Each layer should appear only when you point to its corresponding text, and disappear when you point away from the text.

12   Save and close the page

Unit summary: Rollovers, behaviors, and AP Divs

Topic A   In this topic, you learned about **rollover images**. You learned that rollovers can provide visual feedback for a user's actions and enhance the appeal and interactivity of a page. Then you learned about **behaviors** and applied the Swap Image behavior.

Topic B   In this topic, you learned about the different types of **CSS positioning**, and you learned how to insert **AP Divs**. You learned that any absolutely positioned element is called an **AP element** and appears in the AP Elements panel. You learned how to insert, select, name, resize, and position AP Div layers. You also learned how to dynamically control element **visibility** by applying the Show-Hide Elements behavior.

Independent practice activity

In this activity, you'll create rollover images and apply the Swap Image behavior. Then you'll add AP Divs to a page, insert images in them, position the AP Divs, and apply the Show-Hide Elements behavior.

The files for this activity are in Student Data folder **Unit 4\Unit summary**.

1   Create a site named **Rollovers practice**, using the Outlander folder as the local root folder.

2   Open spiceGallery.html.

3   Click to the right of "Coriander" and press Enter to start a new line.

4   Click the Images : Rollover Images button (in the Common category of the Insert panel).

5   Specify **Cumin** as the image name. For the Original image, specify **cumintext.gif** from the images folder. For the Rollover image, specify **cumintextglow.gif**.

6   Provide alternate text for the image.

7   Below Cumin, add Pepper, using **peppertext.gif** as the Original image, and **peppertextglow.gif** as the Rollover image. Provide alternate text.

8   Apply a Swap Image behavior to the Cumin and Pepper rollovers. Each behavior should replace the spices placeholder image on the page with an image of the appropriate spice when the mouse rolls over the spice's name.

9   Switch to Live View to verify that the rollovers and Swap Image behaviors work as expected, and make modifications if necessary.

10 Close spiceGallery.html.

11 Open heatQuiz.html.

12 Add an AP Div and insert **pepperonicini.gif** into it. (*Hint:* The image is in the heatgraph_images folder, in the images folder.) Name the AP Div **Pepperonicini** and specify the same for the image's alternate text.

13 Add an AP Div and insert **jalapeno.gif** into it. Make **Jalapeno** the AP Div's name and its alternate text.

14 Resize the AP Divs so that they're only as large as they need to be to contain their images.

15 On the heat graph, place the new layers in positions that correspond to their heat values, as shown in Exhibit 4-8. (Overlapping is expected—in the browser, only one image will be displayed at a time.)

16 Select the text **Pepperonicini**. Apply a behavior to show the Pepperonicini layer when the user points to this text, and to hide the layer when the user points away from the text.

17 Apply the same behavior to the Jalapeno text and its corresponding layer.

18 In the AP Elements panel, hide all the spice names so that when you first open the page, the images on the heat graph are not displayed.

19 Test the results in Live View by pointing to the spice names. A spice image should appear only when you point to a spice name.

20 Save and close heatquiz.html.

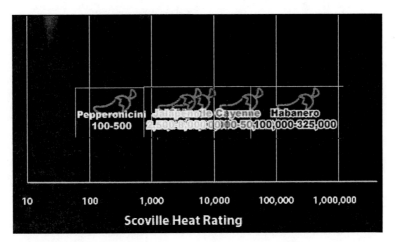

Exhibit 4-8: The position of the AP Div after Step 6

Review questions

1 A rollover is triggered by a(n):

A Behavior

B Up image

C Over image

D Event

2 True or false? The primary and secondary images of a rollover should have the same height and width.

True. The file sizes can be different, but the dimensions of the two images should be identical to prevent distortion and to create a smooth transition between the primary and secondary images.

3 What's the difference between a rollover image and a Swap Image behavior?

With the Swap Image behavior, the trigger object itself doesn't change when you point to it (unless it has been assigned its own rollover).

4 Behaviors are a combination of what two things?

A An event and a user-triggered event

B An event and an action

C An event and a rollover

D A rollover and a swap image

5 Which behavior uses a trigger event to cause changes in one or more other images on the page?

   A Go To URL

   B Swap Image

   C Change Property

   D Pop-Up Menus

6 When you insert an AP Div by using the Draw AP Div button, what HTML tag does Dreamweaver insert?

   A The `<layer>` tag

   B The `<div>` tag

   C The `<divLayer>` tag

   D The `<apdiv>` tag

7 How can you select an AP Div and not its content? [Choose all that apply.]

   A Click the AP Div's selection handle.

   B Click anywhere inside the AP Div.

   C Click the AP Div's border.

   D In the AP Elements panel, click the AP Div's name.

   E Click an edge of the AP Div.

8 To move an AP Div, you can: [Choose all that apply.]

   A Drag from its selection handle.

   B Select its contents and drag.

   C Select it and press an arrow key to move the AP Div one pixel at a time.

   D Point to any border until the pointer changes to a four-headed arrow, and then drag.

9 To make an AP Div appear when a user clicks an object and then disappear when the pointer moves off the object, which events should you use?

   A onMouseOver and onMouseOut, respectively

   B onClick and onMouseDown, respectively

   C onClick and onMouseOut, respectively

   D onMouseUp and onMouseMove, respectively

10 True or false? Setting an AP Div to visible or invisible in the AP Elements panel affects the AP Div only when viewed in Design view, not when viewed in a browser.

   False. Setting an AP Div's visibility in the AP Elements panel applies a CSS style that controls the element's visibility when viewed in a browser.

Unit 5
Working with XML

Unit time: 60 minutes

Complete this unit, and you'll know how to:

A Convert an HTML file to XSLT, bind XML data to an XSLT file, create repeat regions and dynamic links, and attach an XSLT page to an XML document.

Topic A: Applying XML and XSLT

This topic covers the following Adobe ACA exam objective for Dreamweaver CS5.

#	Objective
2.1b	Identify techniques used to maintain consistency.

XML

Explanation

XML (Extensible Markup Language) organizes document elements as data so that you can reuse the content in a variety of formats and applications. It's similar to HTML in that it uses markup tags to organize and display content. Instead of relying on a standard set of predefined tags, however, XML allows you to create your own elements based on what makes sense for your content, as illustrated in Exhibit 5-1. You can then specify what happens to the tagged content in terms of what's published, how it's presented, and so forth.

An XML document is a text file. The elements in it simply provide a semantically meaningful structure for your content.

```
1   <?xml version="1.0" encoding="UTF-8"?>
2   <recipes>
3       <recipe_item id="1">
4           <item>Outlander Chicken</item>
5           <description>This recipe transforms p.
    it in just minutes. Our red chili powder and
6           <link>outlanderchicken.html</link>
7       </recipe_item>
8       <recipe_item id="2">
9           <item>Princely Potatoes</item>
10          <description>A great side dish that c
    as a snack. A touch of garlic give these pot
11          <link>princelypotatoes.html</link>
12      </recipe_item>
13      <recipe_item id="3">
14          <item>Outlander Alfredo</item>
15          <description>Garlic, pepper, and parm
    to your next meal.</description>
16          <link>outlanderalfredo.html</link>
17      </recipe_item>
18  </recipes>
```

Exhibit 5-1: An XML document

XSL and XSLT

For XML data to be displayed meaningfully in a browser, you need to format it with XSL (Extensible Stylesheet Language). XSL formats XML data in much the same way that CSS formats HTML content. You can define styles in an XSL file and then attach it to the XML file. Then, when users access the XML page, it looks the way you defined it in the XSL style sheet.

XSLT (Extensible Stylesheet Language Transformations) is a subset of XSL that allows you to display XML data in a browser by transforming it into HTML. You can create XSLT pages in Dreamweaver and then use them like templates to control page layout and other design attributes.

With XSLT, you can create client-side transformations or server-side transformations. In a server-side transformation, the server does the work of transforming the XML and XSL; in a client-side transformation, the browser does the work. Both methods offer advantages and disadvantages, which are described in the following table.

Method	Advantages	Disadvantages
Client-side transformations	No server configuration is required. Processing is done in the browser.	Not all browsers can execute an XSLT transformation. (However, most current browsers support XSLT.)
		Privacy issues might be involved in delivering XML to the client.
Server-side transformations	There are no browser or device issues because the server does the work.	Integration with a programming language is required, and this increases the complexity of the server configuration.
	Only HTML is delivered from the server; all data is kept private.	

Converting HTML pages to XSLT pages

Although you can create XSLT pages from scratch, you can also convert an HTML page to XSLT and then add XML elements. To convert an HTML page, open it and choose File, Convert, XSLT 1.0. Dreamweaver creates a new XSLT page based on the original HTML page and saves it in the current site folder.

Web applications

Dreamweaver enables you to build rich, interactive Web applications. Web applications interact with data sources like XML documents and databases, reading and writing new information based on user activity and administrative updates. The pages of a Web application are often called *dynamic pages* because the content they deliver might differ from user to user, based on login information, user input, or other variables.

Unlike static pages, which do not change and which display the same information for each user, dynamic pages enable the type of advanced features and functionality commonly found on most commercial Web sites today. Put another way, when a browser requests a static page, that page is delivered as is. When a browser requests a dynamic page, the page is assembled by the application server and then delivered to the user. To create, test, and deploy Web applications, you need an application server, such as ColdFusion, PHP, or ASP.

For example, if you want to build an online bookstore that has an ever-changing inventory, offers membership login, performs secure transactions, and gathers member feedback, you would need to design databases to store that inventory, membership, and transaction data. You would also need to configure an application server, such as ColdFusion, to interact with that data. Then you would build the application pages that put it all in motion.

Web application pages are typically built like templates with editable regions, where the editable regions represent the dynamic areas of the page. When a user requests a page in the browser, the Web server delivers the request to the application server, which processes the request. This process usually involves interaction with a data source and application variables. The application server then delivers the requested information to the user in the form of HTML.

ACA objective 2.1b

Similar to the way CSS enables you to separate your site content from style information, Web applications enable you to separate the framework of your pages from the data they display. This means that a single application template can produce any number of different pages, thereby minimizing ongoing development time and helping to ensure consistency in site presentation and performance.

Do it!

A-1: Converting an HTML page to an XSLT page

The files for this activity are in Student Data folder **Unit 5\Topic A**.

Here's how	Here's why
1 Choose **Site**, **New Site...**	To open the Site Setup dialog box.
2 In the Site Name box, type **Outlander XML**	To name the site.
3 Browse to the current topic folder	Student Data folder Unit 5\Topic A.
Open the Outlander folder, click **Select**, and then click **Save**	To set the root folder for this site and create the site.
4 Open recipes.html	(From the Files panel.) This page contains a brief description of one recipe. You need to add more recipes to the page, and you'll add the content by using XML.
5 Open monthlyrecipes.xml	The page opens in Code view. This XML document contains content for three recipes. The content for each recipe is divided into `<item>`, `<description>`, and `<link>` elements.
6 Switch to recipes.html	You'll convert this HTML page to an XSLT file, which will then transform the XML data into a viewable page.
7 Choose **File**, **Convert**, **XSLT 1.0**	A new XSLT page, titled recipes.xsl, is created and is saved in the site folder.
Locate the new XSL file in the Files panel	(Refresh the file listing if necessary.) A recipes.xsl file has been added to the site files.
8 Close recipes.html	You'll work with the new XSLT page.

Tell students that Web applications are beyond the scope of this course. However, in this unit, students will use XML variables to produce a simple version of a dynamic page.

Students will continue to build the page in the next activity.

Make sure students close the HTML document, not the XSL document.

Binding XML data

Explanation

In a client-side transformation, you add XML data to an XLST page, and a browser does the work of transforming the data into HTML. To add XML data to an XSLT page, you first need to use the Bindings panel to specify the data source.

To specify the XML document to be used as the data source:

1 Choose Window, Bindings to open the Bindings panel.
2 Click the Source link in the upper-right corner of the panel. (Or click the XML link that appears before you link to an XML document.)
3 In the Locate XML Source dialog box, verify that "Attach a local file on my computer or local area network" is selected. (If you're executing a server-side transformation, select the "Attach a remote file on the Internet" option.)
4 Click Browse to open the Locate Source XML for XSL Template dialog box.
5 Navigate to the XML document to which you want to link, select the document, and click OK.
6 Click OK. The schema for the XML document appears as a hierarchy in the Bindings panel, as shown in Exhibit 5-2.

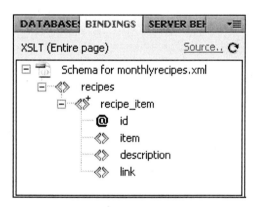

Exhibit 5-2: The Bindings panel

Schema icons

Tell students that they'll learn more about repeating elements later in this topic.

The hierarchy of the schema shows a series of <> bracket icons that represent the elements in the XML document. For example, in Exhibit 5-2, the <> description element is a child element of the <> recipe_item element. Some icons have additional identifiers, such as the plus sign next to the <> recipe_item element. The following table describes the icons that might appear in the schema.

Icon	Description
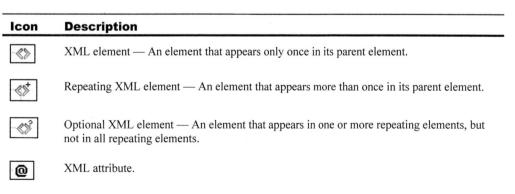	XML element — An element that appears only once in its parent element.
	Repeating XML element — An element that appears more than once in its parent element.
	Optional XML element — An element that appears in one or more repeating elements, but not in all repeating elements.
	XML attribute.

Adding XML elements to a page

After you attach an XML document as a data source, you can add the XML elements to the XSLT page by dragging them from the Bindings panel to the page. When you do this, Dreamweaver inserts XML data placeholders, as shown in Exhibit 5-3. These placeholders are linked to the elements in the XML document. When you open the page in a browser, the placeholders are replaced with the corresponding XML content.

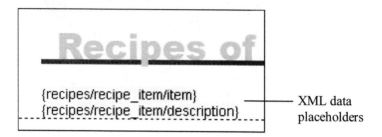
— XML data placeholders

Exhibit 5-3: XML data placeholders in an XSLT page

Formatting XML data placeholders

You can use CSS to format XML data placeholders, similar to the way you format HTML content. Select the placeholder you want to format, and select a style from the Targeted Rule list in the Property inspector.

Do it!

A-2: Binding XML data to an XSLT page

Here's how	Here's why
1 Choose **Window**, **Bindings**	To activate the Bindings panel. You'll bind XML data to the document.
2 In the Bindings panel, click the **XML** link	To open the Locate XML Source dialog box. (You can also click the Source link at the top of the panel.)
3 Verify that **Attach a local file on my computer or local area network** is selected	
4 Click **Browse...**	The Locate Source XML for XSL Template dialog box appears.
Select **monthlyrecipes.xml** and click **OK**	To specify this XML file as the data source for this XSLT page.
5 Click **OK**	

TIPS *Or click the Source link at the top.*

The schema for the monthlyrecipes.xml document is displayed in the Bindings panel.

Be sure that students don't select the monthly recipe graphic.

6 Select all of the recipe text, as shown

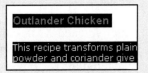

(Don't select the image.) You'll remove this placeholder text and add XML placeholders.

Press DELETE

7 From the Bindings panel, drag the **item** element to the page, as shown

An XML data placeholder that corresponds to the recipe titles appears on the page. You want the recipe descriptions to be just below the titles.

8 Select the **item** placeholder

(If necessary.) Click to select it.

Verify that the selection is formatted as Heading 2

(In the Property inspector.) The recipe items will be formatted as level-two headings.

9 Click to the right of the selection

To place the insertion point to the right of the item placeholder.

Press ↵ ENTER

To add a new paragraph.

10 Drag the **description** element below the item placeholder, as shown

Drag the element from the Bindings panel.

11 Save the page and preview it in your browser

The placeholders are replaced by the XML content. The recipe item text is formatted as a level-two heading.

Close the browser

Working with XML data

Explanation

After you add XML content to an XSLT page, you can manipulate the content in a variety of ways. For example, you can create regions for XSLT documents that work like template regions, or you can generate dynamic links for XML data placeholders that direct users to other pages.

Repeat regions

In some ways, XSLT pages are like template documents. They're linked to XML documents for content, and they provide the styles and layout structure through which the XML content is displayed.

Like templates, XSLT pages can include regions that you can add to streamline the process of adding XML data. For example, if your XML document includes repeating elements, such as those shown in Exhibit 5-4, you can use a *repeat region* to tell a browser to list content automatically within those elements, without your having to manually create placeholders for each of them.

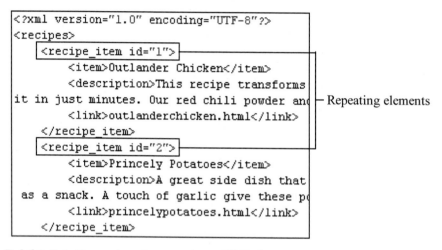

Exhibit 5-4: Repeating elements in an XML document

To add a repeat region to a page:

1. Select the XML data placeholder(s) you want to include in the region.
2. At the top of the Insert panel, select the XSLT category.
3. Click the Repeat Region button to open the XPath Expression Builder dialog box, shown in Exhibit 5-5. (You can also choose Insert, XSLT Objects, Repeat Region.)
4. In the XML schema, select the repeating element that you want to assign to the repeat region. Repeating elements appear with a small plus sign next to them.
5. Click OK. In the XSLT document, a thin border appears around the selected placeholders, and the placeholder text is shortened.

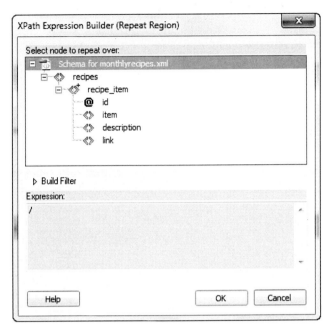

Exhibit 5-5: The XPath Expression Builder dialog box

In Dreamweaver, the repeat region shows only the original placeholders you established earlier. However, when you preview the page in a browser, each instance of the repeating element in the XML document is added to the page.

Do it!

A-3: Creating a repeat region

Here's how	Here's why
1 Drag to select both placeholders	You'll create a repeat region that instructs a browser to display the title and description for the remaining recipes in the XML document.
2 In the Insert panel, select the **XSLT** category	
Click 	(The Repeat Region button.) To open the XPath Expression Builder dialog box.
3 Click **recipe_item**	 To select it. Repeating elements are indicated by a small plus sign.
Click **OK**	A thin, tabbed border appears around the placeholders, and the placeholder text is shortened.
4 Save the page and preview it in your browser	

TIPS *Or hold Shift to select them items.*

TIPS *Remind students that they can press F12 to open the page in Internet Explorer.*

Point out that this is a simple version of a dynamic page, but one that does not require an application server.

Recipes of t

Outlander Chicken

This recipe transforms plain chicken into minutes. Our red chili powder and corian

Princely Potatoes

A great side dish that complements just touch of garlic give these potatoes extra

Outlander Alfredo

Garlic, pepper, and parmesan cheese ma meal.

The other recipes in the XML document are displayed on the page.

Close the browser

Dynamic links

Explanation

You can create links for XML placeholders by using the conventional method of specifying the file path for the link in the Property inspector. If the link resides in a repeat region, however, the same link is applied in each repetition, and this is probably not the desired result. To prevent this, and to take advantage of the flexibility of XML, you can automate the linking process. In the XML document, you can create an element specifically for link information, and then create a dynamic link to the element in the XSLT page. This way, the link in the repeat region changes with each repeating element.

To create dynamic links:

1 Select the XML data placeholder you want to use for the link.
2 In the Property inspector, to the right of the Link box, click the Browse for File icon.
3 In the Select File dialog box, next to "Select file name from," select the Data sources option. The dialog box displays the XML schema for the referenced XML document.
4 Select the schema element that contains the link's file path information.
5 Click OK.

Do it!

A-4: Creating a dynamic link

Here's how	Here's why
1 Deselect the placeholders	(If necessary.) Click anywhere on the page.
Click the **item** placeholder	To select it. You'll create a dynamic link that directs users to the recipe directions when they click the recipe titles.
2 In the Property inspector, click the Browse for File icon	
	(To the right of the Link box.) To open the Select File dialog box.
3 Next to "Select file name from," select **Data sources**	At the top of the dialog box.
4 Select the **link** element	
Click **OK**	
5 Save recipes.xsl	
Preview the page in Internet Explorer	
6 Point to the recipe titles	The titles are now links to corresponding pages.
7 Click **Outlander Chicken**	The browser navigates to the Outlander Chicken recipe page.
Click the Back button	To return to the recipes page.
8 Click the other recipe links	Each link dynamically directs users to the corresponding recipe page.
Close the browser	

Tell students to use the Back button to go back to the recipes page; the navigation links are disabled in these pages.

Attaching an XSLT page to an XML document

Explanation   Although you can preview an XSLT page in a browser, it's ultimately a template for the XML document, which is what users will access after the site is uploaded to a server. To make the XSLT page work correctly on the server side, you need to attach it to the XML document.

To attach an XSLT page to an XML document:

1   Open the XML document for which you want to attach the XSLT page.
2   Choose Commands, Attach an XSLT Stylesheet to open the Attach an XSLT Stylesheet dialog box.
3   Click Browse, locate and select the XSLT page, and click OK.
4   Click OK.

After you attach an XSLT page to an XML document, you can preview the XML document in a browser. The browser uses the attached XSLT document to establish the page layout and styles, similar to the way a CSS style sheet controls the design of an HTML page.

Updating XML content

One advantage of using XML is that you can update page content without having to work directly in the XSLT document. You can better control site integrity because other people, who might not be familiar with the site design, can update the content without the possibility of accidentally changing the layout and styles.

Also, because XML documents are text documents, changes can be made outside of Dreamweaver. After the changes are made in the XML document, you need only to upload the document to the server for the changes to take effect.

Do it!

A-5: Attaching an XSLT page to an XML document

Here's how	Here's why
1 Switch to monthlyrecipes.xml	To view the XML document containing the recipes. You'll attach the XSLT page to this XML document.
Preview the XML document in Internet Explorer	The browser displays the XML elements, color-coded. Raw XML data is not meant for display in a browser. To make sense in a browser, XML content must be formatted with a style sheet.
Close the browser	
2 Choose **Commands, Attach an XSLT Stylesheet**	
3 Click **Browse...**	To open the Select XSLT File dialog box.
Select **recipes.xsl** and click **OK**	Be sure to select recipes.xsl, not recipes.html.
Click **OK**	To close the Attach an XSLT Stylesheet dialog box. Notice that a reference link to the XSLT page appears at the top of the XML document.
4 Save the XML page	
Preview the page in Internet Explorer	Now when you view the page in a browser, it references the XSLT style sheet you created earlier, which provides the formatting for the XML data.
Close the browser	Now you can use the XML document to update page content without working in the XSLT layout.

Be sure that students select recipes.xsl, not recipes.html

5 Place the insertion point as shown

```
<recipe_item id="3">
    <item>Outlander Alfredo<
    <description>Garlic, pe
our next meal.</description
    <link>outlanderalfredo.
```

At the beginning of the description text for the Outlander Alfredo recipe.

Type **Try this lighter version of a creamy classic.**

6 Save the XML file and preview it in your browser	The new content is displayed in the Outlander Alfredo recipe description.
7 Close the browser, and close all open files	

Unit summary: Working with XML

Topic A

In this topic, you learned how to convert an HTML page to an **XSLT page** so that you can incorporate content from an XML document. You also specified the source XML document in the **Bindings panel** and used the schema to add **XML placeholders** to the XSLT page. Then you learned how to create **repeat regions** in an XSLT page so that a browser can display all the repeating elements in an XML document. Finally, you created **dynamic links** and attached an XSLT page to an XML document.

Independent practice activity

In this activity, you'll create a "top-selling products" page that pulls in XML data. You'll convert an HTML page to an XSLT page, and then use the elements in an XML document to provide content.

The files for this activity are in Student Data folder **Unit 5\Unit summary**.

1 Create a site named **XML Practice**, using the Practice subfolder as the local root folder.

2 Open products.html. Convert the HTML page to an XSLT page. Then close the original HTML document.

3 In the Bindings panel, link the topsellers.xml document.

4 Delete the cinnamon content in the left table cell. Remove any formatting applied to the text. Also, delete the price in the right table cell.

5 In the Bindings panel, bind the page to topsellers.xml.

6 Drag the **item** element from the Bindings panel to the left table cell. Set the item placeholder as a level-two heading. (It might be set as a level-two heading automatically.)

7 Click to the right of the item placeholder and press Enter.

8 Drag the **description** element from the Bindings panel and place it under the item placeholder.

9 Drag the **price** element from the Bindings panel and place it under the Price heading in the table. The page should look as shown in Exhibit 5-6.

10 Save the page and preview it in your browser to verify the results. Then close the browser.

11 For the item placeholder, create a dynamic link that references the link element in the XML document. (*Hint:* Select the item placeholder and click the Browse for File icon in the Property inspector. Select Data sources, select the link element in the schema, and click OK.)

12 In the Tag selector at the bottom of the Document window, click the `<tr>` tag to select the entire table row. Create a repeat region for the selected row. (*Hint:* In the XSLT category of the Insert panel, click the Repeat Region icon. Select the product_item repeating element in the schema, and click OK.)

13 Save the page and preview it in Internet Explorer. Click some of the links to test them. Verify that the price data corresponds with each item. When you're finished, close the browser.

14 Link the XSLT page to the XML document. (*Hint:* Open topsellers.xml and choose Commands, Attach an XSLT Stylesheet. Navigate to products.xsl, select it, and click OK.)

15 Save the XML document and open it in your browser to verify the results. When you're finished, close the browser.

16 Close all open documents.

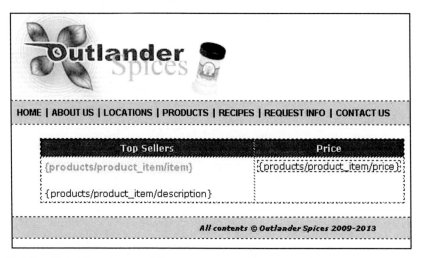

Exhibit 5-6: The item and description placeholders after Step 9

Review questions

1 Which of the following are advantages of client-side transformations? [Choose all that apply.]

A There are no browser or device issues because the server does the work.

B Only HTML is delivered from the server, and all data is kept private.

C Processing is done in the browser.

D No server configuration is required.

2 How can you convert an HTML page to an XSLT page?

A Choose Commands, Convert to XSLT 1.0.

B In the Files panel, right-click the page and choose Rename. Then change the file extension from .html to .xsl.

C Choose File, Convert, XSLT 1.0.

D Right-click anywhere on the page and choose Convert to XSLT 1.0.

3 How can you add a repeat region to an XSLT page? [Choose all that apply.]

A Choose Insert, XSLT Objects, Repeat Region.

B From the Bindings panel, drag a repeating-element icon to the page.

C Right-click where you want to add the region and choose Add Repeat Region.

D In the Insert panel, in the XSLT category, click the Repeat Region icon.

4 How can you create a dynamic link for a selected XML placeholder?

    A Double-click the placeholder. Select the Data sources option; then select a repeating element from the XML schema and click OK.

    B In the Property inspector, click the Browse for File icon. Select the Data sources option; then select a repeating element from the XML schema and click OK.

    C In the Property inspector, enter the file path for the link in the File box.

    D Double-click the placeholder, enter the link's file path in the File box, and click OK.

5 How can you attach an XSLT page to an XML document?

    A Open the XML document and choose Commands, Attach an XSLT Stylesheet. Locate and select the XSLT page, and click OK.

    B In the Files panel, right-click the XSLT page and choose Link to XML. Locate and select the XML document, and click OK.

    C In the Files panel, right-click the XML document and choose Link to XSLT. Locate and select the XSLT page, and click OK.

    D Open the XLST page and choose Commands, Attach an XML Document. Locate and select the XML document, and click OK.

6 Which of the following are advantages of server-side transformations? [Choose all that apply.]

    A There are no browser or device issues because the server does the work.

    B Processing is done in the browser.

    C No server configuration is required.

    D Only HTML is delivered from the server, and all data is kept private.

7 Examples of application servers include: [Choose all that apply.]

    A XSL

    B ColdFusion

    C XML

    D PHP

8 True or false? Dynamic pages are HTML pages that contain client-side scripts for features such as rollovers.

    False. Dynamic pages are assembled by an application server and then delivered to the user. One dynamic page can produce any number of different pages, depending on the user requesting the page and the type of information being requested.

Unit 6

Collaboration and accessibility

Unit time: 45 minutes

Complete this unit, and you'll know how to:

A Use Check In and Check Out to ensure file integrity, attach design notes to files to keep project members informed, and view basic workflow reports.

B Ensure that your Web site meets accessibility requirements, check for missing Alt text, and apply typical usability testing methods.

Topic A: Collaboration

This topic covers the following Adobe ACA exam objectives for Dreamweaver CS5.

#	Objective
2.6	Communicate with others (such as peers and clients) about design and content plans.
4.4f	Identify the purpose and benefits of using InContext Editing.
6.4	Present Web pages to others (such as team members and clients) for feedback and evaluation.
6.5e	Demonstrate knowledge of expanding and collapsing the Files panel to access features such as the site map, get and put, check in and check out, and refreshing the Files panel.
6.5f	Demonstrate knowledge of using file management techniques, such as Subversion control and check-in/check-out, when working in teams.

Check In/Check Out options

Explanation

ACA objective 6.5f

Dreamweaver CS5 provides basic workflow features that you can use to maintain file version integrity, share important notes about files and resources, and view workflow information at a glance. If you're one of a group of people working on a site, the Check In/Check Out Files option provides a way to preserve document integrity by preventing more than one person at a time from working on a file. Dreamweaver displays icons next to file names to help you keep track of your files and their status.

When you check out a file, Dreamweaver displays a green checkmark next to it. If another user checks out a file, a red checkmark appears next to it. You can't edit a file with a red checkmark; the person using the file has to check it back in first. You can right-click a file and choose Show Checked Out By to see who is working on the file.

When you're done editing files and you check them back in, a lock icon appears next to them, as shown in Exhibit 6-1. This icon indicates that the files are read-only. You can't make further changes until you check the files out again.

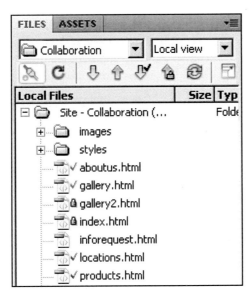

Exhibit 6-1: The Files panel with Check In/Check Out options enabled

To enable the Check In/Check Out system on your Web site:

1 Choose Site, Manage Sites to open the Manage Sites dialog box. (If you're creating a site, choose Site, New Site.)

2 Select the site and click the Edit button to open the Site Setup dialog box.

3 Select the Servers category.

4 Click the plus sign, and type the name of your server in the Server Name box.

5 From the Connect using list, select your connection method.

6 Navigate to your remote site folder and select it.

7 Click Advanced and check "Enable file check out."

8 Enter your name in the Check-out name box, and click Save.

9 Click Save.

To check files in or out, do either of the following:

- If you opted to check out files automatically when you open them, simply double-click a file to check it out. When you check out a file, Dreamweaver replaces the local copy of the document with the remote copy.

- If automatic checkout is not enabled, select the file(s) you want to check in or out, and then click the Check In or Check Out button at the top of the Files panel.

If you've checked a file back in and you decide you don't want to incorporate the changes you made, you can undo them by opening the file and choosing Site, Undo Check Out.

Using Subversion (SVN) with Dreamweaver

ACA objective 6.5f

You can also connect to a Subversion (SVN) server for collaboration and version control. SVN is an open-source version control system that enables workflow collaboration and version tracking so that development teams can work on one code base without having to worry about file versioning and inadvertent edits.

Similar to Dreamweaver's Check In and Check Out process, SVN allows you to check out files, make changes, and check the files back in. You can also use the Ignore command to *cloak* files so that they will not be copied to the server. The SVN system records every change that's made in a file and alerts users when file conflicts arise between team members. If a local copy of a file and the remote copy get out of sync, you can determine the differences between files and synchronize them. With SVN, you can also revert to an older version of a file if necessary.

If a local copy of a file is moved and then checked in, the original file is retained in the original location on the SVN server. Therefore, it's important to avoid moving files unnecessarily and to delete old copies of files that have been moved.

To use Subversion with Dreamweaver, you need to select the Version Control category in the Site Definition dialog box and establish a connection to an SVN server. After the connection is set, you can view the file repository in the Files panel.

Do it!   ## A-1: Checking files in and out

The files for this activity are in Student Data folder **Unit 6\Topic A**.

Here's how	Here's why
1 Choose **Site**, **New Site...**	To open the Site Setup dialog box.
2 Name the site **Collaboration**	
3 Browse to the current topic folder	Student Data folder Unit 6\Topic A.
Open the Outlander folder, and click **Select**	
4 Select the **Servers** category	On the left side of the dialog box.
Click ➕	
In the Server Name box, type **Outlander Server**	You will use a local folder to simulate collaboration on a remote server.
5 From the Connect using list, select **Local/Network**	
Click the folder icon	To open the Choose Folder dialog box.
Navigate up one level	At the top of the dialog box, click the Up One Level button.
Double-click the **Remote site** subfolder and click **Select**	You'll configure this local folder as the "remote" site and enable Check In/Check Out options.
6 Click **Advanced**	At the top of the dialog box.
Check **Enable file check out**	
Verify that **Check out files when opening** is selected	Dreamweaver will automatically check out files when you open them.
7 In the Check-out name box, enter your name	This is the name other users will see when you check out files.
8 Click **Save**	To save your settings.
Click **Save** again	To define the site.

Tell students that they will use a local folder to simulate a remote server. Normally, the remote files would be stored on a server.

ACA objective 6.5f

Tell students that the name and e-mail boxes are optional. If you don't enter a name or e-mail address, other users see just red checkmarks when you check out files.

9 In the Files panel, double-click **index.html**	A dialog box asks if you want to include dependent files, such as images or style sheets.
Click **No**	A dialog box asks if you want to overwrite your local copy of the file.
Click **No**	To close the dialog box and open the page. In the Files panel, a green checkmark appears next to the file, indicating that you've checked it out.
10 Place the insertion point after "Outlander Cooking!"	(The second paragraph in the center column.) You'll add content here.
Press SPACEBAR	
Type **Order your copy online today.**	
11 Save and close index.html, and observe the Files panel	Although you closed the file, it's still marked as being checked out. You need to check in files before other users can open them.
12 In the Files panel, select **index.html**	If necessary.
At the top of the panel, click	(The Check In button.) A dialog box asks if you want to check in dependent files. Because the changes you made in the page were only text, you don't need to check in any dependent files.
Click **No**	To check the file back in. A lock icon appears next to the file. You won't be able to edit the file until you check it out again.
13 Do you or your organization use Subversion for version control?	*Answers may vary.*
If so, what are some advantages to using Subversion (SVN)?	*SVN enables workflow collaboration and version tracking so that development teams can work on one code base without having to worry about file versioning and inadvertent edits. The system records every change that's made in a file and issues an alert when file conflicts arise between team members. It's easy to synchronize files and revert to older versions of files if necessary.*

Tell students that it isn't necessary to include dependent files if the local and remote sites are the same.

Facilitate a brief discussion with a volunteer, if applicable.

ACA objective 6.5f

Design notes

Explanation

ACA objectives 2.6, 6.4

When you're working with a group to develop or maintain a site, you might want to attach notes to files to keep others informed of the changes you've made, request feedback, or simply communicate design and content ideas. You can do this by attaching design notes to files.

To create a design note:

1 Open a file.
2 Choose File, Design Notes to open the Design Notes dialog box, shown in Exhibit 6-2.
3 From the Status list, select a status option for the note.
4 If you want to add the current date to the note, click the small date icon on the right side.
5 In the Notes box, enter your note.
6 If you want users to see the note when they open the file, check "Show when file is opened."
7 Click OK.

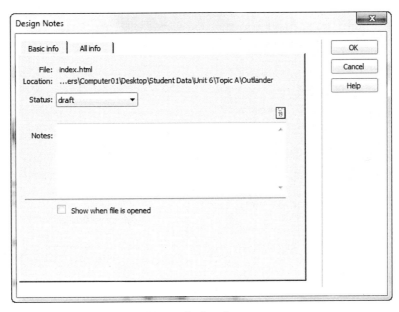

Exhibit 6-2: The Design Notes dialog box

If you opted to show the note when the file opens, the Design Notes dialog box appears whenever the file is opened, even if you work on the file and save it again. If this option isn't selected, users must choose File, Design Notes to preview the notes attached to the file.

Product integration

Design notes are also helpful if you integrate other Adobe products, such as Flash, Fireworks, and Photoshop, into your workflow. When you export a file from one of these programs into a Dreamweaver site, design notes are automatically created that contain references to the original program files.

Do it!

A-2:   Adding a design note

Here's how	Here's why
1 Open locations.html	Dreamweaver automatically checks the file out.
Click **No**	To close the Dependent Files alert box.
2 Choose **File**, **Design Notes...**	To open the Design Notes dialog box.
From the Status list, select **needs attention**	
3 Click the date icon	

ACA objectives 2.6, 6.4

To add today's date to the note.

Click beneath the date, and type **New locations will be official next month. Update when approved.**

4 Check **Show when file is opened**	
Click **OK**	To close the dialog box.
5 Close locations.html	You'll check to make sure the note appears when someone opens the file.
Open locations.html	The Design Notes dialog box appears, showing the note you created.
Clear **Show when file is opened** and click **OK**	To disable the automatic opening of the design note.

Workflow reports

Explanation

When you're working with a team to develop a site, Dreamweaver's workflow reports can show you important information about site files. For example, you can run a report showing all design notes to see what work needs to be done or what actions need to be taken on specific files. Or you can see who has specific files checked out so that you can contact that person if necessary.

To run a workflow report, choose Site, Reports. In the Reports dialog box, under Workflow, check Checked Out By if you want to see which files are checked out and by whom. Check Design Notes if you want to view all design notes throughout the site. Check Recently Modified if you want to see the last modified dates for each site file. When you choose this option, Dreamweaver generates an HTML report and opens it in your default browser.

InContext Editing

ACA objectives 4.4f, 6.4

Adobe InContext Editing is a hosted online service that enables team members and clients to make basic edits using only a Web browser. After you have uploaded your site to the Adobe service, you can invite project members who do not have Dreamweaver—or any experience with Web development—to evaluate the site and make basic content changes. You would simply send users a link to the Adobe hosted site. After they log in, users are presented with simple editing options—no HTML experience is required. InContext Editing is part of the Adobe Business Catalyst service and is especially useful if you want to engage clients in the development and evaluation process.

Do it!

A-3: Creating basic workflow reports

Here's how	Here's why
1 Close locations.html and observe the Files panel	The Files panel shows that the file is still checked out even though it's not open.
2 Choose **Site, Reports...**	To open the Reports dialog box.
From the Report on list, select **Entire Current Local Site**	If necessary.
3 Under Workflow, check **Checked Out By**	
Check **Design Notes**	
Click **Run**	The Site Reports panel opens, showing files that are checked out and the name of the person that has the files checked out. Also, any files with design notes are displayed, along with the note text. This panel enables you to quickly view important information as you collaborate with other team members.

Topic B: Accessibility, usability, and site testing

This topic covers the following Adobe ACA exam objectives for Dreamweaver CS5.

#	Objective
1.4a	Define website accessibility.
1.4b	Demonstrate knowledge of W3C Priority 1 Checkpoints and the W3C Priority 2 POUR principles for making a website accessible.
1.4c	Explain why including accessibility in website design matters to clients and the target audience.
1.4d	Identify elements of an HTML page that can be read by screen readers.
1.5b	Identify page elements that are affected by end-user technical factors, such as download speed, screen resolution, operating system, and browser type.
2.1a	Identify attributes of a website that demonstrate consistency.
2.1b	Identify techniques used to maintain consistency.
2.1g	Demonstrate knowledge of page layout and CSS design decisions that affect how a Web page will print.
2.2a	Identify website elements that are displayed differently on various operating systems and browser versions/configurations.
2.2b	Demonstrate knowledge of page elements that may not appear the same in different browsers.
2.2c	Demonstrate knowledge of the BrowserLab online service for cross-browser compatibility testing.
2.4a	List elements used to improve website usability.
2.4b	Demonstrate knowledge of text formatting guidelines that improve readability.
2.4c	Identify specific techniques used to make a website accessible to viewers with visual and motor impairments.
2.4d	Identify elements of a website that by default are not read by screen readers.
6.1d	Demonstrate knowledge of how to test a website against a storyboard.
6.1e	Demonstrate knowledge of how to test CSS layouts across Web browsers.
6.2a	Demonstrate knowledge of elements involved in conducting a website usability test, such as observation and interviews.
6.3a	Demonstrate knowledge of methods for collecting viewer feedback and site evaluation information to determine if the site meets intended goals and user needs.
6.4	Present Web pages to others (such as team members and clients) for feedback and evaluation.

Accessible content

Explanation

As you create sites, it's important to keep in mind that some people don't use conventional browsers, such as Internet Explorer, Safari, and Firefox. For example, users with visual impairments often use screen readers to access Web site content. It's important that you incorporate basic methods to ensure that your site content is accessible to these users. Doing so can result in sites that are more usable, and it makes your content available to as wide an audience as possible.

ACA objective 1.4c

Section 508 of the U.S. Rehabilitation Act prohibits federal agencies from buying, developing, maintaining, or using electronic and information technologies that are inaccessible to people with disabilities. Sites that comply with Section 508 are accessible on a variety of devices, such as screen readers (which read Web site content aloud), Braille printers, and screen magnifiers.

For your organization and/or clients, it's important that you develop accessible content to comply with these and other related disability laws. Doing so will also allow you to reach as wide an audience as possible.

Accessibility guidelines: Priority 1 checkpoints

ACA objective 1.4a

The World Wide Web Consortium (W3C) publishes a list of guidelines you can use to help ensure that your Web content is accessible. The Web Content Accessibility Guidelines (WCAG) are internationally regarded as the standard for Web accessibility. The guidelines are organized into three categories: Priority 1, Priority 2, and Priority 3. The Priority 1 category guidelines are those that designers *must* follow for their sites to be considered accessible. The Priority 2 guidelines suggest methods that further ensure that content is accessible on alternative devices. Priority 3 guidelines suggest additional methods you might employ.

ACA objectives 1.4b, 2.4a, 2.4c, 2.4d

It's possible that not all checkpoints will pertain to your Web site, depending on the nature and complexity of your content and design. Still, you should be aware of these guidelines, understand why they are important, and incorporate accessibility-related techniques into your markup and design habits. These techniques include:

- Always provide Alt text for all images, image maps and hotspots, sound and video files, other embedded objects, and scripts. Screen readers and other alternative devices cannot access these page elements without text alternatives.

- Structure your content so that it can be read as intended even if style sheets are disabled in the user device. (Alternative devices read pages from top-to-bottom as they appear in the code, not as they are arranged on the page.)

- Ensure that color is not required to convey important information.

- Use the `lang` attribute to indicate the primary language for a Web document. Also, indicate any changes in language within the content.

- Avoid using content that flickers; some types of flickering have been known to cause seizures in some people.

- In tables, identify row and column headers by using the `<tr>` and `<th>` tags, respectively.

- Ensure that content is accessible if scripts or other programmatic elements are not enabled or supported.

- For multimedia content, provide a text description of the important information in the video, audio, or presentation.

- Whenever these basic guidelines cannot be practically met on a given page due to design or technological factors, provide a link to an alternative page that provides equivalent information in text form.

You can read the WGAC Priority 1 checkpoints and delve further into related tips and techniques at `http://www.w3.org/TR/WCAG10/full-checklist.html`.

The POUR principles

In addition to the aforementioned techniques, the guidelines include the acronym POUR to help developers recall four important principles for developing accessible Web sites:

- **Perceivable** — Content must be perceivable.

- **Operable** — Interface components in the content must be operable.

- **Understandable** — Content and controls must be understandable.

- **Robust** — Content should be robust enough to work with current and future user agents (any software or hardware devices that access the Web).

Skip-navigation links

ACA objective 2.4c

In many Web sites, site navigation links are at the top of the page. Screen readers read the first content that appears on the page. If this content is a series of links, the user might have to get through a lot of unnecessary items before he or she can access meaningful content. You can provide *skip-navigation* links (also called "skip to content" links) so that users of screen readers (as well those who use the keyboard instead of a mouse) can navigate directly to the main content of a page.

To create a skip-navigation link, create a named anchor link, in the top-left corner of the page, that links directly to the ID name of your main content section. For example, if your main content is enclosed in a Div with the id "mainContent," you would create a link to #mainContent.

Meaningful heading structures

ACA objectives 2.4a, 2.4c

Skip-navigation links are not the only method of providing users with a way to navigate directly to content. Most modern screen reading devices enable a user to navigate from heading to heading on a page, thereby skipping over navigation links to get to what's important. This means that the way you structure your document headings is important. If a heading is the top heading on a page, define it as an H1. If a heading is a subheading of an H1, use an H2 heading, and so on.

Do it!

B-1: Discussing accessibility guidelines and methods

Questions	Answers
Facilitate a brief discussion for each item. 1 Which set of WCAG guidelines is the baseline standard for accessible content?	*The Priority 1 checkpoints.*
ACA objective 1.4b 2 Name two Priority 1 techniques you can employ to help make your content accessible.	*Answers may vary, but could include:* • *Specifying Alt text for all images, image maps, and image map hotspots* • *Creating table captions* • *Using proper table markup to define table headings and rows* • *Structuring your HTML so that content reads the same whether or not a style sheet is attached* • *Making sure your content is accessible if scripts or other programmatic elements are not enabled or supported*
ACA objective 1.4c 3 Why is it important to create Web sites that are accessible?	*Answers may vary. Creating Web content that is accessible to users with visual or motor impairments is not only the right thing to do, but also helps make your content available to as wide an audience as possible, and it can help build loyalty among your site visitors.*
ACA objective 1.4d 4 What types of content can be accessed by screen readers?	*Answers may vary, but could include:* • *Alt text* • *Table summaries* • *Any text content* • *Page titles*
ACA objectives 2.4a, 2.4c 5 What methods can you use to enable users to skip to your page's main content?	*Create skip-navigation links, and/or use proper heading structures on your pages so that users of screen readers can navigate directly to headings.*

Check for missing Alt text

Explanation

At any time in the site development process, you can quickly check for any instances of missing Alt text on all the pages in your site. This can save you a lot of time and ensure an important aspect of your site's accessibility.

To check for missing Alt text site-wide:

1. Choose Site, Reports to open the Reports dialog box.
2. From the Report on list, select Entire Current Local Site.
3. Under HTML Reports, check Missing Alt Text.
4. Click Run.

The Site Reports panel opens, showing the names of all files that are missing Alt text. Double-click a file name to open the file. The first element with missing Alt text is automatically selected in the code. Add appropriate Alt text to the element, and to any others that need it, and save your changes. When you're done, you can run the report again to verify that the site no longer has any missing Alt text.

Do it!

B-2: Checking for missing Alt text

The files for this activity are in Student Data folder **Unit 6\Topic B**.

Here's how	Here's why
1 Choose **Site, New Site...**	To open the Site Setup dialog box.
2 Name the site **Accessibility**	
3 Browse to the current topic folder	Student Data folder Unit 6\Topic B.
Open the Outlander folder, click **Select**, and then click **Save**	To set the root folder for this site and create the site.
4 Choose **Site, Reports...**	To open the Reports dialog box.
From the Report on list, select **Entire Current Local Site**	If necessary.
Check **Missing Alt Text**	
Click **Run**	The Site Reports panel opens, showing that two files each have an instance of missing Alt text.
5 In the Site Reports panel, double-click **aboutus.html**	To open the file in Split view. The element that is missing Alt text is selected automatically.
| Place the insertion point as shown | ```
height="51" |/></h2>
and manufacturing where
``` |
Type the following code: `alt="Our spices"`	
6 Save and close aboutus.html	
7 Double-click **index.html**	In the Site Reports panel.
Add appropriate Alt text to the selected image	
8 Save and close index.html	
9 Check for missing Alt text again	If there are no other instances of missing Alt text, the Site Reports panel will be empty.
```

Usability considerations

Explanation

An accessible Web site doesn't necessarily equate to a usable Web site. Even if your site meets the technical requirements for accessibility, it might not be an easy site to navigate or to find specific information on. Although ensuring that your content is accessible can improve the overall usability of your site, there are many other factors that affect a site's usability.

Techniques to improve usability

There are many techniques you can use to optimize the usability of your Websites. Some common methods include:

- Write meaningful link text.
- Make sure your site is easily navigable.
- Be consistent.
- Use meaningful document structures.
- Apply color and font styles thoughtfully.
- Make sure your pages load quickly.

Write meaningful link text

ACA objectives 2.4a, 2.4c

The way you write link text (sometimes called link *labels*) can affect both accessibility and usability. Avoid creating links that read "click here." Instead, use meaningful labels that clearly indicate what the user should expect to see on the destination page. For example, "contact us" and "view our sale items" both sufficiently describe the content or purpose of their destination pages.

Make sure your site is easily navigable

Your goal should be to ensure that users can easily find what they're looking for on your site. Simple design choices can have a big impact on this aspect of usability. Start by using a consistent navigation bar on all your site pages to provide global access to each site section or category. For large sites, also provide a site map so that users can get a "big picture" view of the site and easily find each section and individual page.

It's also important to ensure that links are clearly indicated—if you change the default link styles (blue and underlined) to suit your design and color scheme, make sure they still stand out and are easily identifiable as hyperlinks. Consider using CSS hover styles so that link styles change slightly when users point to them.

Be consistent

ACA objectives 2.1a, 2.1b

In addition to consistent navigation, it's important that you keep other repeating elements consistent across pages. For example, don't change the location of page footers or main content sections. Also, use consistent fonts and type styles throughout your site pages.

Use meaningful document structures

Use HTML tags in their proper context to define a meaningful page structure. For example, if you want to create a heading for a page or a section, you should define the text as a heading and not simply change the appearance of the text to *resemble* a heading. The heading level you choose should logically reflect the nature of the content.

Use headings, paragraphs, and other structural elements to organize your pages into a logical hierarchy. Doing so will make your pages more searchable, easier to read, and more accessible to users with alternative browsing devices. Use HTML tables when you need to display tabular data, such as products and prices, because these are typically best presented in structured rows and columns.

ACA objective 2.4a

Also, try to keep the most important information "above the fold," which is a technique from the newspaper industry—information that is considered to be the most important is presented on the front page, above the fold, so that the big headline is quickly visible, even at a glance. You can apply the same concept to a Web page by placing the most important information at the top of the page so that a user does not have to scroll down to view that information.

Apply color and text styles thoughtfully

ACA objectives 2.1g, 2.4b

Use color very carefully and deliberately. In addition to helping to establish the look and feel of your site, color can draw the user's eye to specific content and convey emphasis. The color of your text is especially important. It must be easy to read against its background color, with sufficient contrast to avoid straining users' eyes. It's rarely a good idea to use many different colors; they can be distracting as well as unattractive.

When choosing fonts and type styles, make readability a top priority. Some fonts, such as ornamental serif fonts, are not well suited for the screen and can be difficult to read. Some fonts, such as Georgia and Verdana, are popular and effective options that were designed specifically for readability on screen. Also, choose font sizes, text alignments, and indents that enhance readability rather than detract from it.

It's also important keep the number of font sizes to a minimum because font size can convey structural information. For example, headings have different default font sizes to convey the hierarchical nature of a document's structure.

Your font and color choices will also affect how your pages will print. Background colors, font sizes, and text colors are examples of elements that might not work as well in print as they seem to on screen. You should verify that your design choices work effectively when printed.

Make sure your pages load quickly

ACA objective 1.5b

Perhaps nothing ruins an online experience more than pages that are slow to load. If you keep visitors waiting, they're likely to go elsewhere. Avoid using too many images and multimedia files in a given document, and make sure each image is optimized to keep its file size to a minimum. Also, use an external CSS style sheet to keep your documents free of redundant formatting information and to produce efficient documents with a small file size. The smaller the file size, the faster the page will load.

Usability testing and site feedback

ACA objectives 6.1d, 6.2a, 6.3a

Even after you have carefully considered and applied these and other techniques, it's critical that you conduct a usability test for each site you create before you publish it. Not only do you want to verify that your site is optimally usable and accessible, but you should also seek to verify that your end result meets the goals you set during the planning phase of the site project.

By conducting a usability test, you can determine how successfully your site meets its objectives, see how easy it is for users to find what they're looking for and to use various features, and locate and fix any problems before the site is deployed. Usability testing typically involves project team members plus multiple objective volunteers who are asked to navigate the site and attempt to use its features in several browsers.

A facilitator typically leads test participants through key areas of the site while observing the speed and ease with which users complete specific objectives. User reactions can be monitored and recorded, and post-test interviews can provide further information about the user's experience with the site. Data is then collected and analyzed, and updates and improvements can be made before the site is published.

Continual improvements

Even after you publish a Web site, the feedback and improvement process should continue. It's important that you continually monitor how your site meets the needs of its audience. You can involve users in this process by providing a feedback form that contains both targeted questions and open-ended questions, such as "Tell us what you think about our site" or "How can we improve this Web site?" Or you can simply provide a link in your navigation section that invites users to submit general feedback via e-mail.

Testing layout and design elements in multiple browsers

ACA objectives 2.2a, 2.2b

Before you publish a site, it's important that you test its design and performance because certain elements might be displayed or function differently in various browsers and operating systems. For example, a CSS layout might look different when viewed in Firefox on an Apple computer than it does in Internet Explorer on a Windows PC. Dynamic content or other features dependent upon scripts might also function differently on different systems. By thoroughly testing your pages and making adjustments, you can deliver a reliable and consistent experience for all users.

BrowserLab

ACA objectives 2.2c, 6.1e

You can use BrowserLab to test your site pages as they would appear in different browsers and operating systems. Adobe BrowserLab is a separate application that's part of CS Live, a hosted online service that you can access directly from Dreamweaver. To get started, you need to create a CS Live account. Click the CS Live button in the upper-right corner of the Dreamweaver window and choose "Set up your access to Adobe CS Live online services."

After you have signed up for the service, it's easy to take advantage of the many page preview and testing features of BrowserLab. With a defined site open in Dreamweaver, open the page you want to preview or test. Then click the CS Live button and choose Preview in BrowserLab. BrowserLab compiles the page code and assets and generates side-by-side screenshots of the page as it would look in multiple browsers and platforms. You can even view a transparent overlay of screenshots in order to pinpoint the often subtle layout differences between browsers.

BrowserLab can save you a lot of time and resources because you don't need to set up different test machines and configurations to check your pages in multiple environments.

Do it!

B-3: Discussing usability techniques and feedback

Facilitate a brief discussion for each item.

ACA objectives 2.4a, 2.4b, 2.4c

Questions	Answers
1 Why is it important to use meaningful link text?	*Your link text can affect both accessibility and usability. It should clearly indicate what the user should expect to see on the destination page.*
2 Name three things you can do to improve site usability	*Answers may vary but could include:* • *Write meaningful link text.* • *Make sure your site is easily navigable.* • *Be consistent.* • *Use meaningful document structures.* • *Apply color and font styles thoughtfully.* • *Make sure your pages load quickly.*
3 Name two important factors to consider when choosing colors	*Answers may vary but could include:* • *The overall look and feel of the design* • *How the colors might affect the user's experience* • *How the colors might draw users' eyes to specific content*
4 Name two important factors to consider when styling text	*Answers may vary but could include:* • *The readability of the text* • *The size of the text* • *The number of fonts in use* • *How text styles affect the appearance of the document structure*
5 How can a logical and efficient structure affect usability?	*Documents that are efficiently structured are generally more searchable, easier to read, and more accessible to users with alternative browsing devices such as screen readers.*
6 Why is usability testing a critical aspect of site development?	*Answers may vary. To ensure that your Web site is a success, you need to verify that it's optimally usable and accessible, and that it meets the goals you established for it. The testing process can also reveal problems with code, layout consistency, navigation, and design factors so that you can fix them before publishing the site.*

ACA objectives 6.2a, 6.3a

7 How can you gather ongoing feedback from your users?

On the site, provide a feedback form that contains both targeted questions and open-ended questions, such as "Tell us what you think about our site" or "How can we improve this Web site?" Or you can simply provide a link in your navigation section that invites users to submit general feedback via e-mail.

ACA objectives 2.2c, 6.1e

8 What is BrowserLab and how can it help you to successfully deploy a site?

BrowserLab is a hosted online application that you can sign up for and use to streamline the task of testing your site pages in different browsers and operating systems. This can save a lot of time and resources because you don't need to set up different test machines to verify your results in multiple environments.

Unit summary: Collaboration and accessibility

Topic B   In this topic, you learned how to use the **Check In/Check Out** feature to manage files in a workgroup setting. You also learned how to attach **design notes** to files to facilitate collaboration with team members and keep everyone informed of pending changes or other important items. Finally, you learned how to view **workflow reports**.

Topic C   In this topic, you learned about the importance of ensuring that your pages meet **accessibility requirements**, and you learned how to locate and fix elements that are missing Alt text. Finally, you learned several techniques to improve a site's **usability**, and you learned about typical methods of usability testing and generating site feedback.

Independent practice activity

In this activity, you'll add a design note, search for and fix missing Alt text, and view design notes in the Site Reports panel.

The files for this activity are in Student Data folder **Unit 6\Unit summary**.

1 Create a site named **Practice collaboration**, using the Outlander folder as your local root folder.

2 From the Files panel, open index.html. Attach a design note that indicates a design change you'd like the team to consider making. Set the note to be displayed when the file is opened.

3 Close the file and verify that the design note opens when a user opens that file.

4 Check the site for missing Alt text, and fix all items.

5 Save your changes and close all open files.

6 Run a report to show all design notes in use throughout the site.

7 Close Dreamweaver.

Review questions

1 Which of the following statements are true about files checked out by another user? [Choose all that apply.]

    A Files checked out by another user have a red checkmark next to them.

    B When you open a file that's checked out by another user, a dialog box asks if you want to incorporate that user's changes.

    C You can't edit files checked out by another user.

    D When you open a file that's checked out by another user, it automatically becomes checked out to you, the current user.

2 Which of the following statements are true about design notes? [Choose all that apply.]

    A In documents with design notes applied, the Design Note dialog box always appears when the documents are opened.

    B When adding a design note, you can insert the current date by clicking the small date icon on the right side of the Design Note dialog box.

    C Documents with design notes applied appear with a small checkmark next to them in the Files panel.

    D Design notes provide a simple way for collaborating authors and designers to share notes about a file.

3 How can you view all design notes in a site at once?

    A Choose Site, Reports; under Workflow, check Design Notes; and click Run.

    B Open all site files.

    C Check out all site files.

    D Choose File, Design Notes.

4 What does Section 508 of the U.S. Rehabilitation Act prohibit?

    A It prohibits Web designers from developing, maintaining, or using information technology that's inaccessible to people with disabilities.

    B It prohibits Web designers from developing e-commerce sites without the proper credentials and licensing.

    C It prohibits federal agencies from developing, maintaining, or using information technology that is inaccessible to people with disabilities.

    D It prohibits federal agencies from developing or maintaining sites that aren't accessible in all browsers.

5 How can using design notes be helpful in a workflow environment?

When you're working with a group to develop or maintain a site, design notes can help keep other developers informed of the changes you've made, or provide direction or reminders of changes that need to be made.

Course summary

This summary contains information to help you bring the course to a successful conclusion. Using this information, you'll be able to:

A Use the summary text to reinforce what students have learned in class.

B Direct students to the next courses in this series, if any, and to any other resources that might help students continue to learn about Dreamweaver CS5.

Topic A: Course summary

At the end of the class, use the following summary text to reinforce what students have learned. It's intended not as a script, but rather as a starting point.

Unit summaries

Unit 1

In this unit, students learned about the advantages of using **CSS**. Students learned how HTML and CSS work together to establish a page's design, and they identified the difference between **internal** and **external style sheets** and when to use each type. Students also learned how to define page sections by using **Div tags** and **IDs**, and they learned how to attach an external style sheet to a page. They then learned about the **Box model**, and they applied borders, margins, and padding. Finally, students arranged content sections by applying the **float** and **clear** properties, and they used **Inspect mode** to explore a layout.

Unit 2

In this unit, students created, inserted, and updated **library items**, and they learned how to create and use **code snippets**. Then students learned how to create and edit **server-side includes**, and create and apply **templates**. Students learned how to define editable regions and attributes, create pages from a template, and apply a template to pages that already have content. Finally, students learned how to edit **head content** to improve search engine results, insert **media files**, and edit images.

Unit 3

In this unit, students learned how to create **interactive forms**. Students inserted and edited form **input fields**, such as text fields, textarea fields, lists, menus, check boxes, and radio buttons. Students also learned how to improve the **accessibility** of forms by defining a logical tab order. They then learned how to use **Spry widgets** to create form input fields that validate user entries to ensure the integrity of data. Finally, students used **Live View** to test the results of Spry widgets and other dynamic content.

Unit 4

In this unit, students worked with **rollover images**. Students learned that rollovers can provide visual feedback for a user's actions and enhance the appeal and interactivity of a page. They also learned how to apply **behaviors** to page elements, insert AP Divs and modify their position, size, and visibility, and dynamically control the **visibility** of page elements.

Unit 5

In this unit, students learned how to convert an HTML page to an **XSLT page**. They learned how to **bind XML data** to an XSLT page. Then they learned how to create a **repeat region** in an XSLT page, create dynamic links, and attach an XSLT page to an XML document.

Unit 6

In this unit, students learned how to **check in** and **check out** files to maintain document integrity when working in a group setting, and they learned how to attach **design notes** to files to communicate information to other developers. Students also learned how to create **workflow reports** and locate elements that are missing Alt text. Finally, students learned techniques for ensuring that pages meet **accessibility** and **usability** requirements.

Topic B: Continued learning after class

Point out to your students that it's impossible to learn to use any software effectively in a single day. To get the most out of this class, students should begin working with Dreamweaver CS5 to perform real tasks as soon as possible. We also offer resources for continued learning.

Next courses in this series

This is the last course in this series.

Other resources

For more information, visit www.axzopress.com.

Glossary

AP Div

An absolutely positioned <dig> tag that acts as a generic container to define a content region.

AP element

Any element that's absolutely positioned and appears in the AP Elements panel.

Assets

Components of a Web site, such as images, scripts, and multimedia files.

Behavior

A combination of an event, which is typically triggered by the user, and an action, which occurs in response to the event.

Cascading Style Sheets (CSS)

The standard style language for the Web. While HTML provides the basic structure of a page, CSS controls how the elements within that structure appear in a browser.

Check box

A form input field that allows a user to select multiple items or indicate a yes/no or on/off selection.

Div

A division, or generic container (a <div> tag), that you can use for a variety of purposes.

External style sheet

An external text file that's saved with a .css extension and that contains style rules that define how various HTML elements are displayed.

Layer

Another name for an AP Div.

Library

A special Dreamweaver file you can use to store site assets, such as images, tables, sound files, and video files.

List/Menu

A form input field that displays a list from which the user can select one or more items.

Meta tags

Tags in the <head> section that provide information about the page's content, such as keywords and a description. Meta tags also specify page properties, such as character encoding, the author, or copyright information.

Radio button

A form input field that allows a user to select only one item from a list of items.

Rollover

A technique in which an image is replaced by another image when a user points to it or clicks it. This type of interactivity is popular because it provides visual feedback for a user's actions.

Server-side include

A file that a Web server incorporates into your Web page when a browser requests that page from the server.

Snippets

Sections of code that you can store and retrieve whenever you need them.

Spry widgets

Built-in libraries of HTML, CSS, and JavaScript code that enable you to quickly create interactive components without needing scripting experience.

Tab order

The order in which the insertion point jumps from input field to input field as the user presses the Tab key.

Template

A document you can create and apply to other site pages in order to maintain consistency and make the site creation and maintenance process faster and easier.

Textarea field

A form input field that accepts longer text entries, for such things as user feedback, support questions, and posts in a message board forum.

Text field

A form input field that accepts a single word or short phrase, such as a name or address.

XML (Extensible Markup Language)

A structured language that organizes document components as data so you can reuse the content in a variety of formats.

XSLT (Extensible Stylesheet Language Transformations)

A subset of XSL that lets you display XML data on a page and transform the data into HTML. XSL pages are similar to templates.

Index